It's another Quality Book from CGP

This book is for anyone doing OCR Modular
GCSE Mathematics at Foundation Level.

It contains lots of tricky questions designed
to make you sweat — because that's the only
way you'll get any better.

It's also got some daft bits in to try and make
the whole experience at least vaguely
entertaining for you.

What CGP is all about

Our sole aim here at CGP is to produce the highest quality
books — carefully written, immaculately presented and
dangerously close to being funny.

Then we work our socks off to get them
out to you — at the cheapest possible prices.

Contents

Module 6

Module 7

Published by Coordination Group Publications Ltd.

Editors:
Tim Burne
Simon Little
Ali Palin

Contributors:
Gill Allen
Ruso Bradley
Margaret Carr
Barbara Coleman
JE Dodds
Mark Haslam
John Lyons
Gordon Rutter
Claire Thompson
Ashley Tyson
Lex Ward
Dave Williams
Phillip Wood

With thanks to Janet Dickinson *and*
Charley Darbishire *for the proofreading.*

ISBN-10: 1 84146 574 7
ISBN-13: 978 1 84146 574 6

Groovy website: www.cgpbooks.co.uk

Printed by Elanders Hindson Ltd, Newcastle upon Tyne.
Clipart sources: CorelDRAW® and VECTOR.

Writing and Ordering Numbers

All the questions on this page are for <u>module one</u>...

Q1   Write these numbers as words.

a) 27   ....

b) 507   ....

c) 3,824   ....

Q2   Put these numbers in ascending (smallest to biggest) order.

a) 23   117   5   374   13   89   67   54   716   18

....

b) 1272   231   817   376   233   46   2319   494   73   1101

....

Q3   Write down the value of the number 4 in each of these.

For example   408   *.....hundreds.....*

a) 347   ....   **b)** 41   ....   **c)** 5478   ....

d) 6754   ....   **e)** 4897   ....   **f)** 6045   ....

Q4   Round off these numbers to the nearest 10:

a) 118   ....   **b)** 243   ....   **c)** 958   ....   **d)** 1055   ....

Q5   Round off these numbers to the nearest 100:

a) 627   ....   **b)** 791   ....   **c)** 1288   ....   **d)** 2993   ....

Q6   Look at the following list of numbers:

26   46   25   110   462   31   67   83   113   50

Now write down:

a) The odd numbers   ....   **b)** The even numbers   ....

c) Numbers divisible by 5   ....   **d)** Numbers divisible by 10   ....

Negative Numbers and Temperature

This page is for <u>module two</u> only...

Q1 Write these numbers in the correct position on the number line below:

a) −4   3   2   −3   −5   1

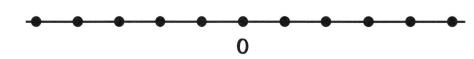

0

b) Which temperature is lower (colder), 8 °C or −4 °C ? ....

c) Which temperature is 1° warmer than −24 °C ? ....

Put the correct symbol, < or >, between the
following pairs of numbers:

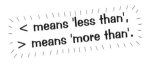
*< means 'less than',
> means 'more than'.*

d) 4   −8

e) −6   −2

f) −8   −7

g) −3   −6

h) −1   1

i) −3.6 −3.7

j) Rearrange the following numbers in order of size, largest first:

−2   2   0.5   −1.5   −8   ....

k) If the temperature is 6 °C but it then gets colder and falls by 11 °C, what is the new
temperature?

....

l) One day in winter the temperature at 0600 was
−9 °C. By midday, it had risen to −1 °C.
By how many degrees did the temperature rise?

....

Always draw a number line to count along, so you can see what you're doing.

Square Numbers and Square Roots

All of this page is for __module three__...

Squares and square roots can look a bit tricky because of the funny symbols...

Remember 6^2 just means "6×6" and $\sqrt{64}$ means the number that __times itself__ is 64.

Q1 Work out the square of these numbers:

a) 1 ....

b) 2 ....

c) 4 ....

d) 8 ....

No calculators for the first 3 questions.

Q2 Find the value of these:

a) $3^2 =$ ....

b) $5^2 =$ ....

c) $6^2 =$ ....

d) $9^2 =$ ....

Q3 Work out the square root of these numbers:

a) 1 ....

b) 9 ....

c) 36 ....

d) 16 ....

Q4 Find the value of these:

a) $\sqrt{25} =$ ....

b) $\sqrt{4} =$ ....

c) $\sqrt{49} =$ ....

d) $\sqrt{64} =$ ....

Q5 Use your calculator to work out the following.
Give your answers correct to 1 decimal place.

a) $\sqrt{2} =$ ....

b) $\sqrt{10} =$ ....

c) $\sqrt{24} =$ ....

d) $\sqrt{40} =$ ....

e) $\sqrt{50} =$ ....

f) $\sqrt{40{,}000} =$ ....

Q6 If a square has an area of 144 cm², what is the length of one of its sides?

....

....

....

Adding and Subtracting

NO CALCULATORS for any of the questions on this page. You'll need to remember the rules for <u>carrying</u> to the left when adding and <u>borrowing</u> from the left when subtracting.

These rather delightful questions are for <u>module one</u>...

Q1   Work out the following additions and subtractions:

a) 63
    +32

b) 75
    +48

c) 28
    +96

d) 31
    +72

e) 18
    +59

f) 36
    −13

g) 45
    −23

h) 81
    −24

i) 25
    − 8

j) 80
    −42

Q2   Fill in the missing digits:

a)   6 5
    + 3□
    ─────
      □□4

b)   7 3
    + 2□
    ─────
      □7

c)   8□
    − □3
    ─────
      4 5

d)   □5
    − 2 7
    ─────
      1□

Now these smashing questions are for <u>module two</u>. Don't be put off by the decimal points. Just remember to put a decimal point in the answer lined up with the ones above.

Q3   Work out these additions and subtractions:

a)   2.4
    +3.2

b) 15.73
    +25.08

c) 26.05
    +72.95

d)   7.34
    + 6.07

e)   3.93
    +9.38

f)   9.8
    −3.1

g)   7.3
    −2.3

h)   6.27
    − 1.56

i)   8.69
    − 3.97

j) 18.63
    − 4.70

 Remember — no calculators on this page.

Q4   Work out how much change Heather should get when she buys:

a) a jar of freeze-dried snails for £3.24 with a £5 note.   ....

b) a packet of earwig sherbet powder for 67p with a £2 coin.   ....

Q5   Work out these missing lengths.

a)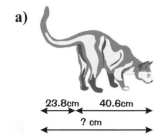

Missing length
is
....

23.8cm   40.6cm
? cm

b)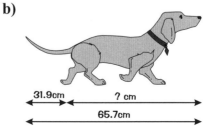

Missing length
is
....

31.9cm   ? cm
65.7cm

Multiplying and Dividing

These first two questions are aimed at <u>module one</u>...

Q1 Do these without a calculator. You'll really need to know your <u>times tables</u>.

a) $3 \times 8 =$ .... **b)** $4 \times 7 =$ .... **c)** $5 \times 9 =$ .... **d)** $6 \times 4 =$ ....

e) $9 \times 8 =$ .... **f)** $7 \times 9 =$ .... **g)** $6 \times 8 =$ .... **h)** $2 \times 9 =$ ....

i) $12 \div 3 =$ .... **j)** $56 \div 8 =$ .... **k)** $63 \div 7 =$ .... **l)** $36 \div 4 =$ ....

m) $36 \div 3 =$ .... **n)** $32 \div 8 =$ .... **o)** $24 \div 4 =$ .... **p)** $45 \div 5 =$ ....

Q2 350 people go to a concert by the oddly-named band "The Hired Sportsmen". Tickets are £7.50 with a £2.50 reduction to ex-athletes. If there are 50 ex-athletes, how much money does the concert take altogether? (You can use your calculator.)

....

The next set of questions are for <u>module two</u>...

Q3 Multiply the following without a calculator:

a) 23×2 **b)** 40×3 **c)** 53×4 **d)** 13×5

= .... = ... = ... = ...

e) 25×4 **f)** 42×3 **g)** 18×2 **h)** 54×3

= .... = ... = ... = ...

Q4 Do these division questions without a calculator:

a) $46 \div 2$ You may wish to set the sum out like this
$$\begin{array}{r} 23 \\ 2\overline{)46} \end{array}$$

b) $86 \div 2$ **c)** $96 \div 3$ **d)** $76 \div 4$

If the numbers don't divide exactly, you'll get a remainder at the end. E.g. $86 \div 8 = 10$ rem 6

e) $85 \div 5$ **f)** $98 \div 6$ **g)** $94 \div 7$

There are lots of different methods for written <u>multiplication</u> and <u>division</u> — it <u>doesn't matter</u> which one you use, as long as you can <u>do it</u> your way.

Multiplying and Dividing

Q5   At a pay-per-stroke animal park, it costs 56p to pat a penguin,
37p to tickle a tortoise and 48p to touch a tiger.

a) Heather pats 6 penguins and tickles a tortoise.
How much will she have to pay?

....

b) How much change will Tim get from a £10 note
if he touches a tiger 17 times?

....

Q6   Abi has £8. Yoghurt-coated mongooses cost 56p.

a) How many mongooses can Abi afford?

....

b) How much change would she get?

....

The rest of the questions on this page are aimed at <u>module three</u>...

When multiplying decimals, ignore the decimal point to start with and just multiply the numbers. Then put the point back in and CHECK your answer looks sensible.

Q7   Multiply these without using a calculator:

a) 3.2 × 4   **b)** 8.3 × 5   **c)** 6.4 × 3

= ....   = ...   = ...

d) 7.1 × 3   **e)** 26.3 × 2   **f)** 2.8 × 7

= ....   = ...   = ...

Q8   Divide these without a calculator.

a) 8.4 ÷ 2   You may wish to set the sum out like this $2\overline{)8.4}^{\,4.2}$

b) 7.5 ÷ 3   **c)** 8.5 ÷ 5   **d)** 26.6 ÷ 7

e) 6.2 ÷ 5   **f)** 2.2 ÷ 4   **g)** 0.9 ÷ 5

Multiplying and Dividing by 10, 100, etc.

This whole page is for <u>module three</u>. And there's <u>no calculators</u> allowed, mister.

Multiplying by 10, 100 or 1000 moves each digit 1, 2 or 3 places to the left — you just fill the rest of the space with zeros.

Q1 Fill in the missing numbers.

    a) $6 \times \boxed{} = 60$ **b)** $0.07 \times \boxed{} = 0.7$

    c) $6 \times \boxed{} = 600$ **d)** $0.07 \times \boxed{} = 7$

    e) $6 \times \boxed{} = 6000$ **f)** $0.07 \times \boxed{} = 70$

Q2 **a)** $8 \times 10 = $ ....   **b)** $34 \times 100 = $ ....   **c)** $52 \times 100 = $ ....

    d) $9 \times 1000 = $ ....   **e)** $436 \times 1000 = $ ....   **f)** $0.2 \times 10 = $ ....

    g) $6.9 \times 10 = $ ....   **h)** $4.73 \times 100 = $ ....   **i)** $3.51 \times 1000 = $ ....

Q3 For a school concert chairs are put out in rows of 10.
How many will be needed for 16 rows? ....

Q4  How much do 100 chickens cost? ....

£2.99 EACH

Dividing by 10, 100 or 1000 moves each digit 1, 2 or 3 places to the right.

Q5 **a)** $30 \div 10 = $ ....   **b)** $43 \div 10 = $ ....   **c)** $5.8 \div 10 = $ ....

    d) $423 \div 100 = $ ....   **e)** $228.6 \div 100 = $ ....   **f)** $61.5 \div 100 = $ ....

    g) $296 \div 1000 = $ ....   **h)** $60 \div 1000 = $ ....   **i)** $6334 \div 1000 = $ ....

Q6 Blackpool Tower is 158 m tall. If a model
of it is built to a scale of 1 : 100, how tall
would the model be?

....

Q7 A factory produces action dolls of the famous extreme-adventurer Tim B.
If 1000 dolls weigh 2.1kg, what is the weight of one Tim B doll in g?

....

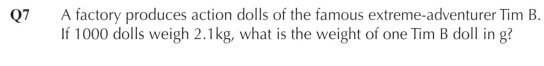

What's crazy Tim doing now...

Fractions, Decimals and Percentages

This circle is divided into two equal parts — each bit is 1/2 of the whole.

The questions below are for <u>module one</u>.

Q1   What fraction is shaded in each of the following pictures?

a)   **b)**   **c)**   **d)**

....

Q2   Try these <u>without</u> a calculator:

a) 1/2 of £30 = ...   **b)** 1/4 of £20 = ...

c) 1/4 of £16 = ...   **d)** 3/4 of £16 = ...

Q3   Shade in the correct number of sections to make these diagrams equivalent.

$\dfrac{1}{2}$ =

$\dfrac{1}{4}$ =

For this second part, you need to shade so that <u>1 out of every 4</u> parts are shaded.

These questions are for <u>module two</u>.

Q4   **a)** Write down 25% as a fraction. ....   **b)** What's 1/2 as a percentage? ....

c) What's 0.25 as a percentage? ....   **d)** What's 3/4 as a decimal? ....

Q5   Answer these without a calculator:

a) 50% of £12 = ...   **b)** 25% of £20 = ...

c) 25% of £48 = ...   **d)** 50% of £68 = ...

Q6   The residents of Scraggy End were asked in a survey which was their favourite speciality local meat. The results are shown in the bar.

a) Which was the most popular meat?

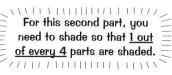

....

b) What percentage chose this meat?   **c)** What percentage preferred penguin meat?

....

Fractions, Percentages and Decimals

More __module two__ questions...

Q7 The pie chart shows the results from the phone vote at the 2006 Scraggy End Animal Karaoke competition. There were 128 votes altogether.

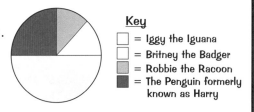

Key
☐ = Iggy the Iguana
☐ = Britney the Badger
▨ = Robbie the Racoon
■ = The Penguin formerly known as Harry

a) Which animal received 50% of the votes?

....

b) What percentage of the total votes did The Penguin formerly known as Harry receive?

....

c) How many votes did these animals receive:

i) Iggy the Iguana ....

ii) Britney the Badger? ....

Finally, here are some completely animal-free __module three__ questions...
No calculators for these questions.

Q8 Find the following "fractions of quantities":

a) 1/8 of 32 = ... ÷ 8 = ...   **b)** 1/10 of 50 = ... ÷ 10 = ...

c) 1/12 of 144 = ... ÷ .... = ...   **d)** 1/25 of 75 = ... ÷ .... = ...

Q9 Now try these: Eg. 2/5 of 50   50 ÷ 5 = 10   2 × 10 = <u>20</u>

a) 2/3 of 60   60 ÷ 3 = ...   2 × .... = ...

b) 4/5 of 25   25 ÷ .... = ...   4 × .... = ...

c) 6/9 of £1.80   .... ÷ .... = ... × .... = £ .... or .... p

d) 10/18 of £9.00   .... ÷ .... = ... × .... = £ ....

e) 2/3 of one day (24 hours)   .... ÷ .... = ... × .... = ... hours

f) 5/6 of one year (12 months)   .... ÷ .... = ... × .... = ... months

g) 2/5 of one kilogram (1000 grams)   .... g

Q10 Find these "percentages of quantities":

a) 10% of £50 ....   **b)** 5% of £50 = ...

c) 30% of £50 = ...   **d)** 10% of 90 cm = ...

e) 10% of 4.39 kg = ...   **f)** 15% of 200 kg = ...

Time

These questions are for <u>module one</u>.

Q1   Fill in the missing times. The first one has been done for you.

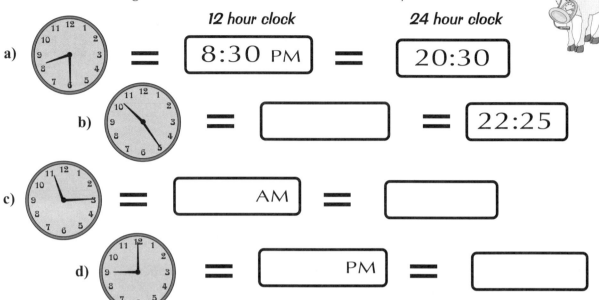

	12 hour clock		24 hour clock

a) = 8:30 PM = 20:30

b) = [ ] = 22:25

c) = AM = [ ]

d) = PM = [ ]

Q2 a) How long is it from 7.30am to 11.35am? ....hours............minutes.

b) How long is it from 8.45am to 12.15pm? ....hours............minutes.

c) How long is it from 0.00am to 1.25pm? ....hours............minutes.

Jolly good. Now the following questions are aimed at <u>module three</u>.

Q3   Tim, Kate and Ed have a competition to see who can say the phrase "this biscuit has fluff on it" the most slowly. Tim and Ed both start the phrase at 3.40 pm.

a) Ed completes the phrase at 5.48 pm. How long did he take? ....

b) Tim takes 3 hrs 32 mins to say the phrase. At what time did he finish? ....

c) Kate takes 190 minutes, finishing at 10.36 pm. When did she start? ....

Q4   The timetable below refers to three trains that travel from Asham to Derton.

a) Which train is quickest from Asham to Derton? ....

b) Which train is quickest from Cottingham to Derton?

....

c) I live in Bordhouse. It takes me 8 minutes to walk to the train station. At what time must I leave the house by to arrive in Derton before 2.30 pm? ....

Asham – Derton			
	Train 1	Train 2	Train 3
Asham	0832	1135	1336
Bordhouse	0914	1216	1414
Cottingham	1002	1259	1456
Derton	1101	1404	1602

Number Patterns

The questions on this page are for __module one__ and __module two__...

Q1　Draw the next two pictures in each pattern.
How many match sticks are used in each picture?

a)

....　　.......　　.......　　　.......　　　　.......

b)
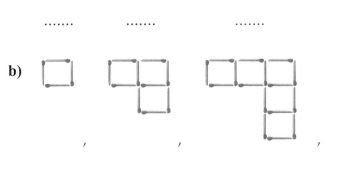

....　　.......　　　.......　　　.......　　　.......

Look for patterns in the numbers as well as pictures.

Q2　Look for the pattern and then fill in the next three lines. Some of the answers are too big to fit on a calculator display so you must spot the pattern.

a)

7×6 = 42

67×66 = 4422

667×666 = 444222

6667×6666 = ...

66667×66666 = ...

666667×666666 = ...

b)

$1 \times 81 = 81$

$21 \times 81 = 1701$

$321 \times 81 = 26001$

$4321 \times 81 = 350001$

$54321 \times 81 =$ ....

$654321 \times 81 =$ ....

$7654321 \times 81 =$ ....

Q3　In each of the questions below, write down the next three numbers in the sequence and write the rule that you used.

Once you've worked out the next numbers, go back and write down exactly what you did — that will be the rule you're after.

a) 1, 3, 5, 7, ..., ..., ... Rule ....

b) 3, 7, 11, 15, ..., ..., ... Rule ....

c) 3, 30, 300, 3000, ..., ..., ... Rule ....

d) 2, 4, 8, 16, ..., ..., ... Rule ....

12

Formulas and BODMAS

If module one, advance to page 14. If you pass go, collect £200. If _module two_ or _module three_, go to Q1.

Q1 Here is a formula for working out the value of y: | Multiply x by 2, then add 10 |
Work out the value of y when x = 12.

....

Q2 A gardener uses the following formula to calculate how much he charges, in pounds:

> *Multiply the number of hours worked by 6, then add 5*

How much would the gardener charge for 5 hours work? ....

Q3 The famous extreme-adventurer Tim B runs one-way trips to the moon. The cost for a group to travel is:

> *Number of people in group × £5.99*

How much would it cost for a group of 10 people to travel to the moon?

....

These next few questions are just for _module three_. Remember **BODMAS**? That's the funny little word that tells you the order for working formulas out.

Q4 If x = 3 and y = 6 find the value of the following expressions.

a) $x + 2y$ ....
c) $4(x + y)$ ....
e) $2x^2$ ....

b) $2x \div y$ ....
d) $(y - x)^2$ ....
f) $2y^2$ ....

Q5 If $V = u + at$, find the value of V when u = 8, a = 9.8 and t = 2. ....

Q6 The cost, C pence, of hiring a taxi is $C = 100 + 25n$, where n is the number of miles you travel in it. Find C when:

a) n = 2 ....
b) n = 10 ....
c) n = 15 ....

Q7 The cost of framing a picture, C pence, depends on the dimensions of the picture. If $C = 10L + 5W$, where L is the length in cm and W is the width in cm, then find the cost of framing:

a) a picture of length 40 cm and width 24 cm ....

b) a square picture of sides 30 cm. ....

Equations

This splendid page is for <u>module three</u> only. Some people have all the luck.

You're spoilt for choice when solving equations — you can use "<u>Common Sense</u>", "<u>Trial and Error</u>" or even the "<u>Proper Way</u>". Just make sure you pick your favourite method and get lots of practice at using it.

Q1   Solve these equations:

a) $3 + f = 7$ b) $a + 6 = 20$ c) $b + 12 = 30$ d) $48 + c = 77$

....

Q2   Solve these equations:

a) $g - 7 = 4$ b) $h - 14 = 11$ c) $i - 38 = 46$ d) $l - 7 = -4$

....

Q3   Solve these equations:

a) $4m = 28$ b) $7n = 84$ c) $15p = 645$ d) $-5s = 35$

....

Q4   Solve these equations:

a) $\dfrac{t}{3} = 5$ b) $u \div 6 = 9$ c) $\dfrac{v}{11} = 8$ d) $\dfrac{y}{-3} = 7$

....

Coordinates

This page is for __module one__.

Q1   On the grid plot the following points. Label the points A,B...
Join the points with straight lines as you plot them.

A(0,8) B(4,6) C(4.5,6.5) D(5,6) E(9,8) F(8,5.5) G(5,5) H(8,4) I(7.5,2) J(6,2) K(5,4)
L(4.5,3.5) M(4,4) N(3,2) O(1.5,2) P(1,4) Q(4,5) R(1,5.5) S(0,8).

You should see the outline of an insect. What is it? ....

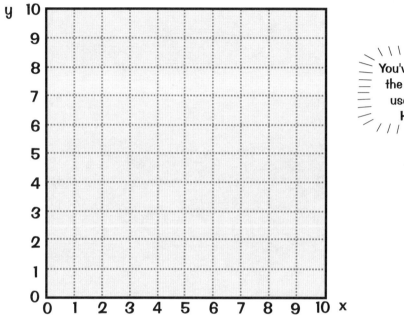

You've got to get your coordinates in the right order — or they're totally useless — you always go IN THE HOUSE then UP THE STAIRS.

Q2   Write down the letter which is by each of the following points.
The sentence it spells is the answer to question one.

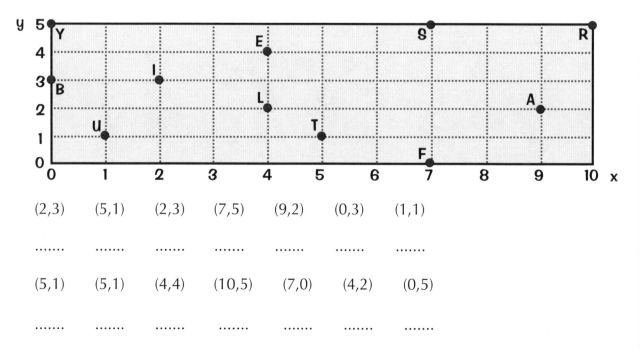

(2,3)   (5,1)   (2,3)   (7,5)   (9,2)   (0,3)   (1,1)

....

(5,1)   (5,1)   (4,4)   (10,5)   (7,0)   (4,2)   (0,5)

....

Conversion Factors

These questions are for <u>module one</u> (but they're still worth doing for modules two & three).

Q1 Express each quantity in terms of the unit given in the brackets:

a) 4.5 mm (cm) .... **c)** 3010 mm (m) ....

b) 3456 cm (m) .... **d)** 0.12 m (mm) ....

Q2 Neil is a large alien. His Earth Membership Card states his height as 2.92 m.

What is his height in centimetres? ....cm

Now these two questions are for <u>module two</u>...

Q3 Express each quantity in terms of the unit given in the brackets:

a) 4.32 kg (g) .... **b)** 450 g (kg) ....

Q4 Health and Safety rules at Tommy's Tomato factory say the maximum weight anyone is allowed to lift by themselves is 20 kg. Tommy has three piles of tomatoes weighing 11300 g, 7014 g and 1204 g.

a) What is the total weight of the tomatoes? .... kg.

b) Is Tommy allowed to lift all three piles of tomatoes at once?

....

Finally <u>module three</u>. Crank up that volume. Oh, different sort of volume. Sorry.

Q5 A large jug can hold 4 litres of liquid.

a) How many millilitres is this? ....ml

The jug is only a fifth full.

b) How many litres are of liquid are in the jug? l

c) How many millilitres is this? ....ml

Don't forget that if you're unsure which to use, <u>multiply</u> AND <u>divide</u> by the conversion factor... then see which is the sensible answer.

Reading Scales and Estimating

This question is for <u>module one</u>...

Q1   Read the following scales. You'll need to add units to any answers which don't have them.

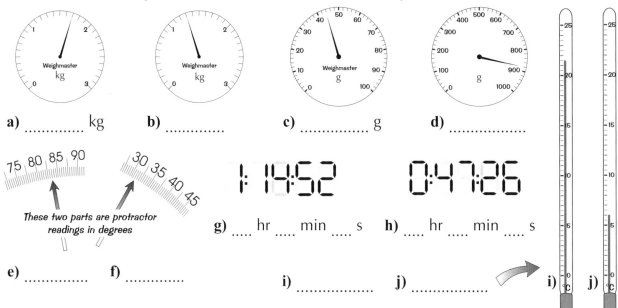

a) .... kg   **b)** ....   **c)** .... g   **d)** ....

These two parts are protractor
readings in degrees

g) ..... hr ..... min ..... s   **h)** ..... hr ..... min ..... s

e) ....   **f)** ....   **i)** ....   **j)** ....   **i)** °C   **j)** °C

Ah, the joys of reading scales... and now for some <u>module two and three</u> fun...

Q2   Estimate the following lengths then measure them to see how far out you were:

OBJECT	ESTIMATE	ACTUAL LENGTH
a) Length of your pen or pencil	....	....
b) Width of your thumbnail	....	....
c) Height of this page	....	....
d) Height of the room you are in	....	....

Q3

The ranger is almost 2 m tall.
Estimate the height of the
giraffe in metres.

....

If you have trouble estimating the height by
eye, try measuring the ranger against your
finger. Then see how many times that bit of
finger fits into the height of the giraffe.

Estimating Angles

Estimating angles is easy once you know the 4 special angles —
you can use them as reference points.

90°   180°   270°   360°

This page is for _module two_.

For each of the angles below write down its type, estimate its size (before you measure it!) and finally measure each angle with a protractor. The first one has been done for you.

Angle	Type	Estimated Size	Actual Size
a	acute	40°	43°
b			
c			
d			
e			
f			

a

b

c

d

e

f

Drawing Angles

This page is for <u>module two</u>.

These instruments are used to measure angles.

An angle measurer.

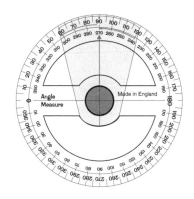

A protractor.

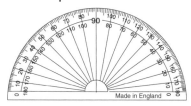

Don't forget protractors have two scales — one going one way and one the other... so make sure you measure from the one that starts with 0°, not 180°.

Q1 Use an angle measurer or protractor to help you to draw the following angles.

a) 20°   **b)** 65°   **c)** 90°

d) 136°   **e)** 225°   **f)** 340°

Q2 a) Draw an acute angle and measure it.   **b)** Draw an obtuse angle and measure it.

Acute angle measures ....°   Obtuse angle measures ....°

c) Draw a reflex angle and measure it.

Reflex angle measures ....°

Perimeter and Area

This page is for __module one__.

__Perimeter__ is the __distance around__ a shape. __Area__ is how much __space__ the shape covers.

Q1 Find the perimeter of these shapes (you may need to work out some of the lengths):

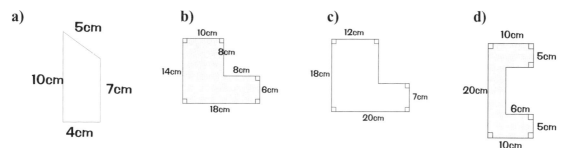

a) Perimeter ....

b) Perimeter ....

c) Perimeter ....

d) Perimeter ....

Q2 Both of the shapes below are made up of squares. Each square has an area of 0.5cm².

a) What are the areas of these shapes in cm²?

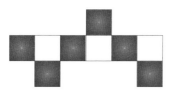

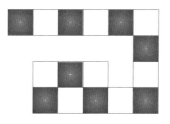

....

b) Complete the body for the man-eating caterpillar.
The extra body you draw should have an area
of 13 cm². Each square has an area of 1 cm².

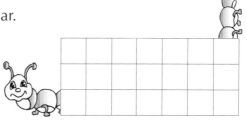

Q3 Trendy Trev the disco pig has left his footprint on some graph paper.
Each square represents 1cm².

Estimate the area of Trev's footprint:

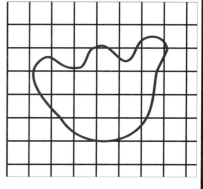

Area: ....

Volume

THIS PAGE IS ALL <u>*MODULE ONE*</u>*... Oops, sorry. Wrong volume. I'll turn it down a bit ...*

Q1 Each shape has been made from centimetre cubes. The volume of a centimetre cube is 1 cubic cm. How many cubes are there in each shape? What is the volume of each shape?

a)

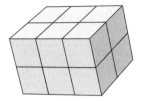

There are ...... cubes.
The volume is
...... cubic cm.

b)

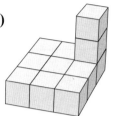

There are ...... cubes.
The volume is
...... cubic cm.

c)

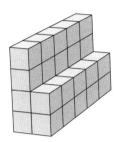

There are ...... cubes.
The volume is
...... cubic cm.

d)

There are ...... cubes.
The volume is
...... cubic cm.

e)

There are ...... cubes.
The volume is
...... cubic cm.

f)

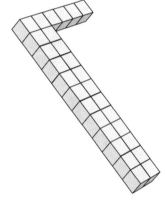

There are ...... cubes.
The volume is
...... cubic cm.

g)

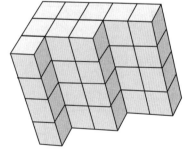

There are ...... cubes.
The volume is ...... cubic cm.

h)

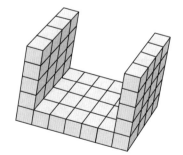

There are ...... cubes.
The volume is ...... cubic cm.

You simply add up the cubes... but make sure you don't miss any —
remember that there are some rows at the back too.

Shapes You Need to Know

a shape with lots of sides

A polygon is ~~a dead parrot~~. A regular polygon has all sides the same length and all its angles are the same. This page is for <u>module one</u>.

Q1 Name these regular shapes.

a)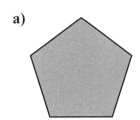

b)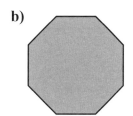

c)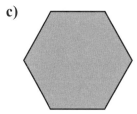

....

Q2 Draw these regular shapes.

a) An equilateral triangle

b) A hexagon

A good starting point for these is a circle drawn with a pair of compasses

Q3 Measure the diameter, radius and circumference of SuperStan's white eye.

a) Diameter = ...

b) Radius = ...

c) Circumference = ...

Measure the circumference with a piece of string.

Q4 Draw a circle with radius 2.5cm.
On your circle label the circumference, a radius and a diameter.

Solids, Nets and Projections

A net is simply a solid shape folded out flat. But to confuse things, many shapes like a cube have <u>lots</u> of different possible nets.

These questions are for <u>module two</u>.

Q1 Which of the following nets would make a cube?

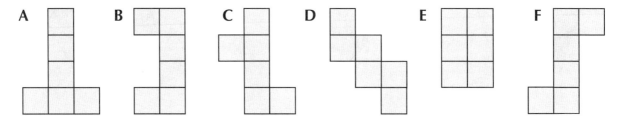

A   B   C   D   E   F

Q2 Below is a sketch of a cuboid and its net. The net is drawn to scale but not finished: it needs two more faces. Draw them in the correct position.

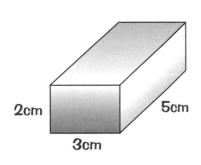

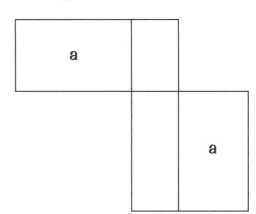

And some <u>module three</u>...

Q3 This unfinished isometric drawing shows a cuboid with dimensions 1 cm by 4 cm by 3 cm.

a) Complete the isometric drawing of the cuboid.

b) Draw the front elevation, side elevation and plan of the cuboid in the space below.
Make sure your drawings are to scale.

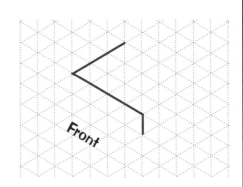

OCR Modular Maths — Modules 1, 2 and 3

Symmetry

Now for more <u>module two</u>. I'm beginning to sound like a broken record..

Q1 These shapes have more than one line of symmetry.
Draw the lines of symmetry using dotted lines.

a)

b)

c)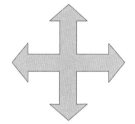

Q2 Some of the letters of the alphabet have lines of symmetry.
Draw the lines of symmetry using dotted lines.

A B C D E F G H I J K L M

N O P Q R S T U V W X Y Z

Q3 Complete the diagrams below so that the dashed line is the only line of symmetry.

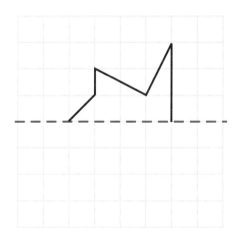

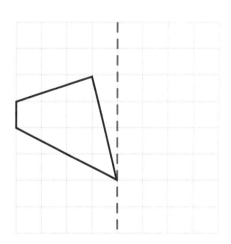

MIRROR LINE = LINE OF SYMMETRY = AXIS OF SYMMETRY —
they'll use all of these words, but they mean the same thing.

Maps and Directions

This page is for <u>module one</u>.

Q1

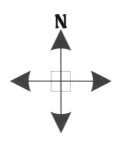

Start at the dot shown and draw lines by following
the directions. What shape have you drawn?

....

a) West 4 squares.

b) North 4 squares.

c) East 4 squares.

d) South 4 squares.

e) North East through 2 squares.

f) North 4 squares.

g) South West through 2 squares.

h) West 4 squares.

i) North East through 2 squares.

j) East 4 squares.

Q2

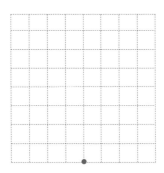

Joe's house

Shop

Church

Sue's house

Park

Jane's house

a) What direction does Jane go to get to Sue's house? ....

b) What direction is the church from Joe's house? ....

c) What is South East of Sue's house? ....

d) What is West of Sue's house? ....

e) Jane is at home. She is going to meet Sue in the park. They are going to the shop and
then to Joe's house. Write down Jane's directions.

....

To remember the compass directions, there's always "<u>Never Eat Shredded Wheat</u>" or you
could make up your own — <u>Not Everyone Squeezes Wombats</u>, <u>Nine Elves Storm Wales</u>...

Maps and Directions

Remember this great way of remembering what order to read grid references:

First <u>A</u>cross the bottom, <u>T</u>hen <u>U</u>p the side. <u>FAT</u> Unicorn.

This is all for <u>module two</u> by the way.

Q3   Below is a map of Damcoster town centre.

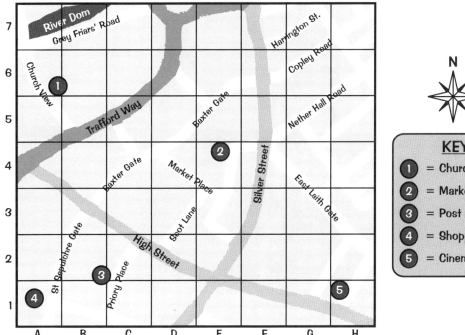

KEY
①　= Church
②　= Market
③　= Post Office
④　= Shopping Centre
⑤　= Cinema

a) What compass direction is the market from the shopping centre?

....

b) Ric walks East from the market. When he reaches Silver Street, he walks North East up the street and takes his first left. He then takes his second left. What street is he now standing upon?

....

c) A group of tourists at the post office want to know where they can get a cappuccino and blueberry muffin. Give them directions to the coffee morning at the local church.

....

....

....

....

d) What is the grid reference of the cinema?

....

Scale Drawings

This whole page is for <u>module three</u>, and it's nothing to do with sketching fish.

Q1 The scale on this map is 1 cm : 4 km.

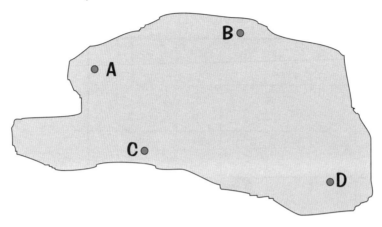

a) Measure the distance from A to B in cm. ....

b) What is the actual distance from A to B in km? ....

c) A helicopter flies on a direct route from A to B, B to C and C to D.
What is the total distance flown in km?

....

Q2 The shape below on the left is a plan for a funky layout for a new pond in a garden.
The drawing has been done to a scale of 1cm : 1m.

a) How long is the real-life length of the path labelled **"a"** ? ....

b) The designer wants a drawing to a new scale so starts one (top right) at 2cm : 1m.
Complete this drawing.

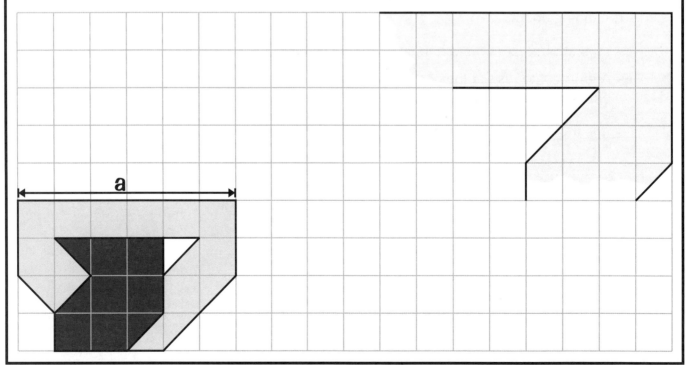

Transformations — Enlargements

The scale factor is a fancy way of saying HOW MUCH BIGGER the enlargement is than the original. A scale factor of 2 means that the enlargement is twice the size of the original.

This question is for __module one__ — things can only get bigger from here.

Q1 Draw an enlargement of this shape. Make each side 4 times as long.

Now these questions are for... __module three__.

Q2 What is the scale factor of each of these enlargements?

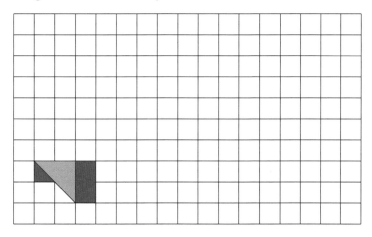

Just pick one of the sides and see how many times longer it is.

A: Scale factor is .... **B:** Scale factor is .... **C:** Scale factor is ....

Q3 Enlarge this shape using scale factor 3.

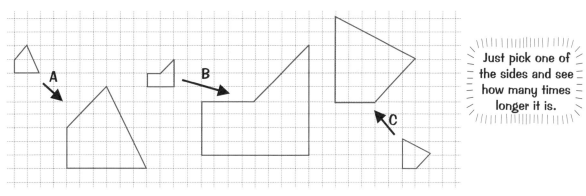

Conversion Graphs

The same method can be applied to all conversion graphs. From the number you want to convert go straight upwards (or across) until you hit the line, then change direction and read off the number you end up at. Jack-a-nack-a-nory!

This page is for module three.

Q1 This graph can be used to convert the distance (miles) travelled in a taxi to the fare payable (£). How much will the fare be if you travel:

a) 2 miles ....

b) 5 miles ....

c) 3 miles? ....

How far would you travel if you paid:

d) £5 ....

e) £11 ....

f) £6.50? ....

Q2 80 km is roughly equal to 50 miles. Use this information to draw a conversion graph on the grid below. Use the graph to estimate the number of miles equal to:

a) 20 km ....

When you've got to draw your own conversion graph, your best bet is to work out a few different values, and mark them on the graph first.

b) 70 km ....

c) 90 km ....

Q3 How many km are equal to:

a) 40 miles ....

b) 10 miles ....

c) 30 miles ....

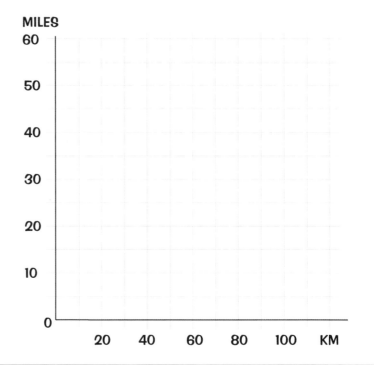

Probability

Probability is just about <u>working out the chances</u> of different things happening. And there's a fair chance it'll come up in the Exam, so have a go at these questions.

These questions are for <u>module one</u>.

Q1 Bert has 8 pairs of socks — 6 yellow pairs, 1 blue pair and 1 red pair. He picks a pair at random. Write down whether these events are impossible, unlikely, evens, likely or certain.

a) The pair of socks is blue. ....

b) The pair of socks is yellow. ....

c) The pair of socks is green. ....

Q2 I roll a fair six-sided dice. Choose the right word to complete the following sentences.

impossible   certain   likely   evens   unlikely   fair

a) It is .... that I roll a number between 1 and 6.

b) It is .... that I roll an odd number.

Q3 Ali P the inept crocodile-wrestler has three crocodiles to wrestle — Chris, Craig and Crystal.

Complete the table to show all the possible orders in which she could wrestle the crocodiles. The first order is done for you.

You might not need to use all the lines.

Chris	Craig	Crystal

The next two questions are for <u>module two</u>...

Q4 Mika and Nick play a game of pool. The probability of Nick winning is 7/10 and the probability of Mika winning is 3/10.

a) Put an arrow on the probability line below to show the probability of Nick winning. Label this arrow N.

b) Now put an arrow on the probability line to show the probability of Mika winning the game. Label this arrow M.

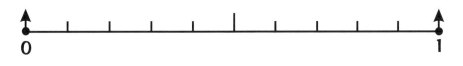

Probability

Q5 Put an arrow on the probability line to show the following.
Also explain why you've put your arrow there:

a) The probability that I choose a red disc from a bag
containing 6 red discs and 4 purple discs.

> More than half the discs are red, so you know straight away that the arrow should be more than halfway along.

0 ——————————|—————————— 1

EXPLAIN: ....

b) The probability that Elvis Presley will release a new number one record.

0 ——————|—————— 1

EXPLAIN: ....

You've guessed it — these are what you need if you're doing __module three__.

When you're asked to find the probability of something, __always check__ that your answer is between 0 and 1. If it's not, you know straight away that you've made a mistake.

Q6 A bag contains ten balls. Five are red, three are yellow and two are green.
What is the probability of picking out:

a) A yellow ball? ....

> Probability of yellow = number of yellows ÷ total number.

b) A red ball? ....

c) A green ball? ....

d) A red or a green ball? ....

e) A blue ball? ....

Q7 Write down the probability of these events happening:

a) Throwing an odd number with a six-sided dice. ....

b) Drawing a black card from a pack of playing cards. ....

c) Drawing a black King from a pack of cards. ....

d) Throwing a prime number with a six-sided dice. ....

Q8 A selection box contains 10 bars of chocolate. 6 are milk chocolate, 2 are dark chocolate and 2 are white chocolate. What is the probability that a bar picked at random contains:

a) Dark chocolate? ....   **b)** Milk chocolate? ....

c) On the scale shown, mark with an arrow
the probability that the bar isn't white chocolate.

0 ——————|—————— 1

Averages

The first half of this page is for __module two__ and __module three__.

To find the __mode__ and __median__ put the data in order of size first — then it's easier to see which number you've got __most of__ and to find the __middle value__.

Q1 Find the mode for each of these sets of data.

a) 3, 5, 8, 6, 3, 7, 3, 5, 3, 9,

.... Mode is ....

b) 52, 26, 13, 52, 31, 12, 26, 13, 52, 87, 41

.... Mode is ....

Q2 Find the median for these sets of data.

a) 3, 6, 7, 12, 2, 5, 4, 2, 9

.... Median is ....

b) 14, 5, 21, 7, 19, 3, 12, 2, 5

.... Median is ....

If you're doing module two, it's time for a well earned rest. For those of you doing __module three__, here are some questions on __mean__ and __range__.

Q3 Find the mean of each of the sets of data below. If necessary, round your answers to 1 decimal place:

a) 13, 15, 11, 12, 16, 13, 11, 9 = ...

> Remember the formula for mean —
> total of the items ÷ number of items.

b) 16, 13, 2, 15, 0, 9 = ...

c) 80, 70, 80, 50, 60, 70, 90, 60, 50, 70, 70 = ...

Q4 Find, __without__ a calculator, the __mean__ and __range__ for each of these sets of data:

a) 5, 3, 7, 3, 2 = ...

b) 7, 3, 9, 5, 3, 5, 4, 6, 2, 6 = ...

Q5 The number of goals scored by a hockey team over a period of 10 games is listed below.

0, 3, 2, 4, 1, 2, 3, 4, 1, 0.

What is the range of the number of goals scored? ....

Tables, Charts and Graphs

These two pages are for <u>module one</u> and <u>module two</u>.

Make sure you read the questions <u>carefully</u>. You don't want to lose easy marks by looking at the wrong bit of the table or chart.

The first four questions are for <u>module one</u>.

Q1 Dirk took his temperature and recorded it on this graph. What was his temperature at:

a) 10am? ....

b) 2pm? ....

c) What was his highest temperature?

....

d) When was this? ....

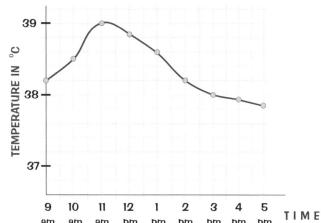

Q2 Here is a horizontal bar chart showing the favourite colours of a class of pupils.

a) How many like blue best? ....

b) How many more people chose red than yellow? ....

c) How many pupils took part in this survey? ....

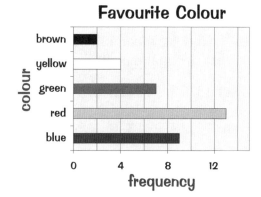

Q3 This pictogram shows the favourite drinks of a group of pupils.

Favourite Drinks	Number of Pupils
Lemonade	✧ ✧ ✧ ✧ ✧ ✧ ✧ ✧
Coke	✧ ✧ ✧ ✧ ✧ ✧ ✧ ✧ ✧ ✧
Tango	✧ ✧ ✧ ✧ ✧ ✧
Orange Squash	✧ ✧ ✧
Milk	✧

✧ Represents 2 pupils.

a) How many pupils were questioned? .... pupils.

b) How many pupils prefer non-fizzy drinks? .... pupils.

Tables, Charts and Graphs

Q4 The table below shows the average daily hours of sunshine for the winter months in the Costa del Sol.

MONTH	October	November	December	January	February	March
SUN HOURS	7	6	5	6	6	8

Complete the pictogram to represent the information. Use your own symbol.

Month	Hours of Sunshine
October	

.... represents .... hour(s) of sunshine.

Module two — you're back in the game.

Q5 One hundred people were asked in a survey what colour eyes they had.
Use this two-way table to answer the following questions.

a) How many people in the survey had green eyes? ....

b) How many women took part in the survey? ....

c) How many women had blue eyes? ....

d) How many men had brown eyes? ....

	Green eyes	Blue eyes	Brown eyes	Total
Male	15			48
Female	20		23	
Total		21		100

Q6 This table shows the prices for a one-week penguin watching holiday in three places.

a) How much will I pay if I choose the Argentina holiday, and start my week on 15th October?

....

b) Where will I be going if I start my holiday on 28th October, and it costs me £3000?

....

Start Date	Price per person (£)		
	Argentina	Antarctica	Dulton Zoo
1 Sept - 30 Sept	1000	2400	100
1 Oct - 31 Oct	1200	3000	90
1 Nov - 30 Nov	2000	3500	90
1 Dec - 31 Dec	3000	4000	60

c) I decide on Argentina or Antarctica, sometime between 1st November and 31st December. If I want to pay no more than £2500, where should I go? ....

d) After spending an unexpectedly large amount on Christmas decorations, I'm forced to change my plans. Calculate the total cost for myself and two friends to go on the Dulton Zoo holiday in December. ....

Tally / Frequency Tables

This page is for <u>module three</u> only.

Q1 At the British Motor Show 60 people were asked what type of car they preferred. Jeremy wrote down their replies using a simple letter code.

Saloon - S   Hatchback - H   4x4 - F   MPV - M   Roadster - R

Here is the full list of replies.

H	S	R	S	S	R	M	F	S	S	R	R
M	H	S	H	R	H	M	S	F	S	M	S
R	R	H	H	H	S	M	S	S	R	H	H
H	H	R	R	S	S	M	M	R	H	M	H
H	S	R	F	F	R	F	S	M	S	H	F

Fill in the tally table and add up the frequency in each row. Draw the bar chart of the results.

TYPE OF CAR	TALLY	FREQUENCY
Saloon		
Hatchback		
4 × 4		
MPV		
Roadster		

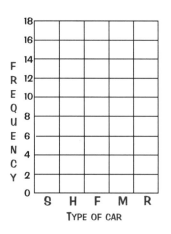

Q2 Here is a list of marks which 32 pupils gained in a History test:

65	78	49	72	38	59	63	44
55	50	60	73	66	54	42	72
33	52	45	63	65	51	70	68
84	61	42	58	54	64	75	63

Complete the tally table making sure you put each mark in the correct group, and fill in the frequency column. Then draw the bar chart of the results.

MARKS	TALLY	FREQUENCY
31-40		
41-50		
51-60		
61-70		
71-80		
81-90		
	TOTAL	

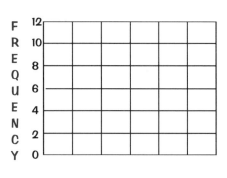

Always cross out each thing as you tally it, so there's no chance you'll count it twice.

Times and Divide without a Calculator

There are lots of written methods you can use for multiplication and division. What you have to do is <u>pick a method</u> you like and <u>practise using it</u> on questions until you know it like the inside of your armour.

Q1 Use written methods to multiply the following:

no calculators!!

a) 23 × 2 **b)** 225 × 3 **c)** 546 × 5

= .... = ... = ...

d) 126 × 14 **e)** 413 × 26 **f)** 309 × 61 **g)** 847 × 53

= .... = ... = ... = ...

Q2 Now use written methods to deal with these little blighters:

a) 834 ÷ 3 **b)** 645 ÷ 5 **c)** 702 ÷ 6

d) 1000 ÷ 8 **e)** 595 ÷ 17

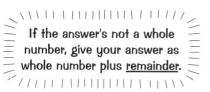
If the answer's not a whole number, give your answer as whole number plus <u>remainder</u>.

f) 768 ÷ 16 **g)** 996 ÷ 24 **h)** 665 ÷ 14

Decimals with a Calculator

Decimals often come up in "real life" questions. For money questions, you might need to turn the calculator display into money, e.g. 2.35 becomes £2.35. Or for some questions, you might have to round a decimal answer to a whole number.

You can use your calculator for all the questions on this page.

Q1 a) At Johnnie's Cheap and Nasty Cheese Mart you can get 135 g of cheese for £1.
How much cheese would you get for £35.50? Give your answer in kg.

....

b) Johnnie decides to make some more expensive cheese to sell at his mart.
This cheese costs £13.25 for 742 g. How much cheese is this per £1?

....

Q2 After an all night Astronomy and Rockets Society Event, the organisers decide to put on buses to take home the 556 sleepy astronomers.

a) If each bus can take 30 astronomers,
how many buses will be needed?

....

> Be careful with division questions like this —
> the answer needs rounding to a whole number,
> but you need decide whether to round up or down.

b) If they use double decker buses, which hold
45 people, how many will they need?

....

Q3 Razza and Shazza are training for the Great North Run. Razza runs 3.5 miles
in 30 minutes. How far will she run if she keeps up this pace for:

a) 1 hour   **b)** 2 hours   **c)** 127 minutes

....

Shazza takes 6.23 minutes to run 1 mile. At this pace, how long would she take to run:

d) 3.28 miles   **e)** 6.55 miles   **f)** 13.1 miles

....

Q4 At an Indian Cuisine Restaurant, Simon the Extreme Spicy Food Eater orders 3 vegetable
vindaloos at £4.95 each, 1 pilau rice for £2.25 and 2 naan breads for £2 each.

a) If Simon came with £35, how much money does he have left to spend now?

....

b) Simon suddenly wants to order as many soothing "lassi" drinks as possible.
If lassi drinks cost £3.00 each, how many can Simon afford with the money he has left?

....

Decimals without a Calculator

Put your hands up slowly and step away from the calculator! Now lie face down on the floor and don't move. (I.e. no calculators on this page.)

Q1 Put these numbers in order of size — from the smallest to the largest.

a) 3.42   4.23   2.43   3.24   2.34   4.32

....

b) 6.7   6.704   6.64   6.642   6.741

....

Always look at the whole number part first, then the first digit after the decimal point, then the next etc.

c) 1002.8   102.8   1008.2   1020.8   108.2

....

Q2 Work out these additions and subtractions:

a)   4.3
    +7.7

b)   56.31
    +83.29

c)   7.78
   − 6.46

d)   6.48
   − 2.87

e)   15.20
   − 8.73

Count the number of d.p.s in the question and put the same number into your answer.

Q3 Multiply these without using a calculator:

a) 6.3×24

b) 28.4×5

c) 16.9×3.5

= ....

= ....

= ....

d) 13.4×0.32

e) 3.3×2.7

f) 0.42×3.53

= ....

= ....

= ....

Q4 Aisha visits her local garden centre. How much change does she need when she buys:

a) 5 slug-eating wallabies for £3.50 each with a £20 note.

....

b) 3 wallaby-eating slugs for £2.60 with a £10 note?

....

Fractions, Decimals and Percentages

Q1   Change these fractions to decimals:

a) $\frac{1}{2}$ ....

b) $\frac{3}{4}$ ....

c) $\frac{7}{10}$ ....

d) $\frac{19}{20}$ ....

e) $\frac{1}{100}$ ....

f) $\frac{3}{8}$ ....

g) $\frac{2}{1000}$ ....

h) $\frac{1}{3}$ ....

Q2   Change these fractions to percentages:

a) $\frac{1}{4}$ ....

b) $\frac{3}{10}$ ....

c) $\frac{4}{5}$ ....

d) $\frac{12}{25}$ ....

e) $\frac{8}{100}$ ....

f) $\frac{2}{40}$ ....

g) $\frac{7}{8}$ ....

h) $\frac{11}{30}$ ....

Q3   Change these decimals to percentages:

a) 0.62 ....

b) 0.74 ....

c) 0.4 ....

d) 0.9 ....

e) 0.07 ....

f) 0.02 ....

g) 0.125 ....

h) 0.987 ....

Q4   Change these percentages to decimals:

a) 25% ....

b) 49% ....

c) 3% ....

d) 30% ....

Q5   Change these percentages to fractions:

a) 75% ....

b) 60% ....

c) 15% ....

d) 53% ....

Q6   Change these decimals to fractions:

a) 0.5 ....

b) 0.8 ....

c) 0.19 ....

d) 0.25 ....

e) 0.64 ....

f) 0.06 ....

g) 0.125 ....

h) 0.075 ....

 A FRACTION IS A DECIMAL IS A PERCENTAGE —
they're all just different ways of saying "a bit of" something.

Multiples and Factors

The multiples of a number are its times table — if you need multiples of more than one number, do them separately then pick the ones in both lists.

Q1 What are the first five multiples of:

a) 4? ....

c) 12? ....

b) 7? ....

d) 18? ....

Q2 Find a number which is a multiple of:

a) 2 and 6 ....

c) 2 and 3 and 7 ....

b) 7 and 5 ....

d) 4 and 5 and 9 ....

Factors multiply together to make other numbers.
E.g. $1 \times 6 = 6$ and $2 \times 3 = 6$, so 6 has factors 1, 2, 3 and 6.

Q3 a) I am a factor of 24.
I am an odd number.
I am bigger than 1.
What number am I?

....

b) I am a factor of 30.
I am an even number.
I am less than 5.
What number am I?

....

Q4 A perfect number is one where the factors add up to the number itself.
For example, the factors of 28 are 1, 2, 4, 7 and 14 (not including 28 itself).
These add up to $1 + 2 + 4 + 7 + 14 = 28$, and so 28 is a perfect number.

Complete this table, and circle the perfect number in the left hand column.

Number	Factors (excluding the number itself)	Sum of Factors
2		
4	1, 2	3
6		
8		
10		

The sum of the factors is all the factors added together.

Q5 a) What is the biggest number that is a factor of both 42 and 18 (i.e. the highest common factor)?

....

b) What is the smallest number that has both 4 and 18 as factors?

....

Prime Numbers

Basically, prime numbers don't divide by anything (except 1 and themselves).
5 is prime — it will only divide by 1 or 5. 1 is an exception to this rule — it is not prime.

Q1   Write down the first ten prime numbers. ....

Q2   Give a reason for 27 not being a prime number. ....

Q3   Using any or all of the figures **1, 2, 3, 7** write down:

   a) the smallest prime number ....

   b) a prime number greater than 20 ....

   c) a prime number between 10 and 20 ....

   d) two prime numbers whose sum is 20 .... , ...

   e) a number that is not prime. ....

Q4   Find all the prime numbers between 40 and 50. ....

Q5   In the <u>ten by ten square</u> opposite,
ring all the prime numbers.

   The first three have been done for you.

1	②	③	4	⑤	6	7	8	9	10
11	12	13	14	15	16	17	18	19	20
21	22	23	24	25	26	27	28	29	30
31	32	33	34	35	36	37	38	39	40
41	42	43	44	45	46	47	48	49	50
51	52	53	54	55	56	57	58	59	60
61	62	63	64	65	66	67	68	69	70
71	72	73	74	75	76	77	78	79	80
81	82	83	84	85	86	87	88	89	90
91	92	93	94	95	96	97	98	99	100

Q6   A school ran three evening classes: <u>judo, karate and kendo</u>.
The judo class had 29 pupils, the karate class had 27 and the kendo class 23.
For which classes would the teacher have difficulty dividing the pupils into equal groups?

   ....

Q7   Find three sets of three prime numbers which add up to the following numbers:

   10 ...., ..., ...   29 ...., ..., ...   41 ...., ..., ...

Ratio Questions

I think I can spot a Golden Rule lurking here...
DIVIDE FOR ONE, THEN TIMES FOR ALL.

Q1 In 'The Pink Palace' the walls are painted a delicate shade of pink by mixing 2 tins of red paint to every 3 tins of white paint.

Write this as a ratio.

Red tins to White tins =

.... : ....

Q2 In 'The Penguin Palace' the walls are painted a beautiful black and white pattern.
Black and white paint are used in the ratio 5:3.
How much black paint would be needed with:

a) 6 litres of white? ....

b) 12 litres of white? ....

c) 21 litres of white? ....

Q3 I have some friends coming round for dinner and want to cook my favourite fish pie.
My recipe serves 4 people, but I will need enough pie for 9 people.

a) How many potatoes will I need to cook my fish pie for everyone?

....

b) How much haddock will I need?

....

c) If eggs come in boxes of 6, how many boxes should I buy?

....

....

....

RECIPE FOR MY
FAVOURITE FISH PIE

400 g haddock
8 large potatoes
1 tin mushy peas
12 eggs
1 pinch of salt
2 tb/spoons curry powder

Trial and Improvement

Remember — the key to all trial and improvement questions is to find two <u>opposite cases</u>. Then you just try numbers in between until you find the right answer. Groovy.

Q1   Use the trial and improvement method to write down the number I first thought of in each of these:

a) I multiply by 3 and then take away 5.
The answer is 19.

My number was ....

b) I add 10 then double the number.
The answer is 26.

My number was ....

c) I half it then add 9. The answer is 24.

My number was ....

d) I divide by 5 then add 12. The answer is 32.

My number was ....

e) I subtract 15 then divide by 3. The answer is 20.

My number was ....

Q2   Now try this:
I think of a number, multiply it by itself, add 5, divide by 2 then add 10. The answer is 25.

My original number was ....

Making Formulas

This page is free from artificial colours, flavours and preservatives. But, alas, not from penguins...

Q1 The total number of CDs owned by two friends is given by:
Number of CDs owned by Chloe, x, + number of CDs owned by Sadiki, w.
Write down a formula for the total number, N, of CDs they own. ....

Q2 A zookeeper uses the following formula to work out the number of fish he needs to buy to feed his penguins each week:

Number of penguins —— (× 30)—(+ 20) ——▶ Number of fish

Write this formula connecting F and P, where F is the
number of fish needed and P is the number of penguins. ....

Q3 Write a formula for:

a) The perimeter, P, of a square which is equal to the side length, d, multiplied by 4.

....

b) The area, A, of a rectangle which is equal to the length, l,
multiplied by the width, w.

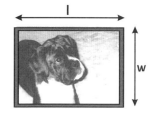

....

c) Use the formula in b) to calculate the area of a rectangle with l = 6 cm, w = 3.5 cm.

....

Q4 A pizza place runs a special deal. Each time you eat there you get a token, and when you've collected enough tokens you get a free pizza. The relationship between number of tokens and number of free pizzas is shown in the table below.

Number of Tokens (t)	10	20	30	40	50
Number of free pizzas (p)	1	2	3	4	5

Think about what the subject of the formula should be. Here it makes more sense for it to be pizzas — so p = ...

a) Write down a formula connecting the number of
free pizzas (p) with the number of tokens (t). ....

b) The chefs at the pizza place are paid according to how long they've worked there.
This table shows the relationship between number of years worked and pay per hour:

Number of years worked (y)	1	2	3	4	5
Pay — pounds per hour (p)	7	8	9	10	11

Write down a formula connecting pay
per hour (p) and years worked (y). ....

Number Sequences

Once you've worked your way through these questions, have a look back at __page 11__ for more questions on finding and continuing number patterns.

Q1 The rule for a sequence is '*multiply the previous term by 2 and add 5*'.
The first term of the sequence is 2.

a) Work out the second term of the sequence. ....

b) Calculate the fifth term of the sequence. ....

Q2 In this sequence the rule for getting each term is '*double n and add 1*'.
Complete the table to give the first 8 terms of the sequence.

n	1	2	3	4	5	6	7	8
t	3	5						

Q3 The letter n describes the position of a term in the sequence. For example,
if n = 1, that's the 1st term…if n = 10 that's the 10th term and so on.
In the following, use the rule given to generate (or make) the first 5 terms.

a) 3n + 1, when *n* = 1, 2, 3, 4 and 5
produces the sequence ...., ..., ..., ..., ...

b) 5n – 2, when *n* =1, 2, 3, 4 and 5
produces the sequence ...., ..., ..., ..., ...

c) n^2, when n = 1, 2, 3, 4, and 5
produces the sequence ...., ..., ..., ..., ...

Q4 The nth term of a sequence is given by: 2n – 2.

a) Write down the third term of the sequence. ....

b) Write down the tenth term of the sequence. ....

Q5 In the following number patterns, write down the next 3 terms:

a) 2, 5, 8, 11, ..., ..., ...

b) 7, 12, 17, 22, ..., ..., ...

c) 1, 11, 21, 31, ..., ..., ...

d) 49, 56, 63, 70, ..., ..., ...

Q6 These are the first four terms in a sequence: 2, 4, 8, 16,...

a) Write down the fifth term. ....

b) Write down the seventh term. ....

Travel Graphs and Speed

To calculate speed from a distance/time graph, divide the distance by the time.
To help remember this, think of the units.
Miles per hour, means miles divided by hours, which is distance divided by time.

Q1 The graph shows Nicola's car journey from her house to Alan's house, picking up Robbie on the way.

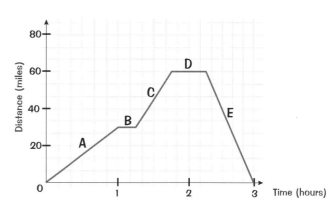

a) If Nicola started her trip at 10.00 am at what time did she return home? ....

b) How far is Robbie's house from Nicola's? ....

c) How long did they stop at Alan's for? ....

d) During which section was the speed greatest? ....

e) How long did the return journey take? ....

f) What was the speed of the car during section E? ....

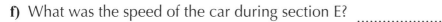

You can work out where the houses are by looking for the flat parts of the graph — the bits where Nicola stops. There are two flat parts here — one for Robbie's house and one for Alan's.

Q2 The travel graph shows the journey of a boy going on a run.

a) Between what times was the boy running the <u>fastest</u>?

....

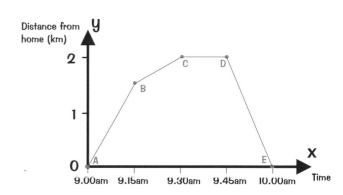

b) Calculate his <u>fastest speed</u> in km/hr.

....

c) For how long was the boy <u>resting</u>?

....

d) What happened to the boy's speed at <u>B</u>?

....

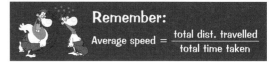

Remember: Average speed = total dist. travelled / total time taken

e) How <u>far</u> did the boy run?

....

f) What was the <u>average speed</u> for his entire run?

....

Interpreting Graphs

A whole page of graph questions and the good news is there's not a single point to be plotted. These questions are about understanding what the graphs are showing.

Q1 The following graph was presented to show the increase in Carbon Dioxide in our atmosphere. Give two reasons why it is misleading:

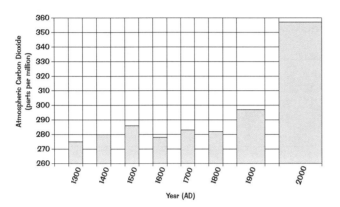

1) ....

....

....

2) ....

....

....

Q2 Match the following graphs with the statements below:

a) The cost of hiring a plumber <u>per hour</u> including a <u>fixed call-out fee</u>. ....

b) <u>Exchange rate</u> between Euros and American Dollars ....

c) <u>Speed against time</u> for a car travelling at constant speed. ....

d) The <u>area of a circle</u> as the radius increases. ....

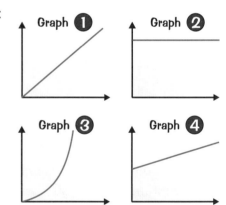

Q3 Water is poured into each of these containers at a <u>constant rate</u>.

Match the containers to the graphs showing the <u>depth</u> of water (d) against <u>time</u> (t) taken to fill the container.

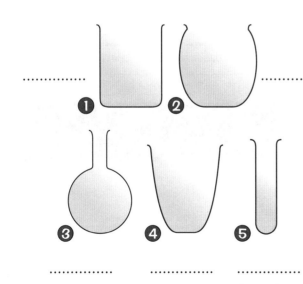

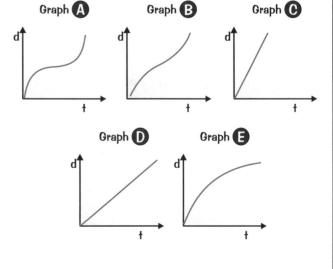

Metric and Imperial Units

You'd better learn ALL these conversions
— you'll be well and truly scuppered without them.

APPROXIMATE CONVERSIONS

1 kg = 2.2 lbs	1 gallon = 4.5 l	1 inch = 2.5 cm
1 litre = 1.75 pints	5 miles = 8 km	1 foot = 30 cm

Q1 Change each of these weights from kilograms to pounds.

10 kg = ... lbs   16 kg = ... lbs   75 kg = ... lbs

Change each of these capacities in gallons to litres.

5 galls = ... l   14 galls = ... l   40 galls = ... l

Q2 The water butt in my garden holds 20 gallons of rain-water. How many litres is this?

....

Q3 Tom walked 17 km in one day, while Dave walked 10 miles. Who walked further?

....

....

It doesn't matter which distance
you convert — but here it's easier
to convert David's miles to km.

Q4   A recipe for a gigantic chocolate cake requires 8 lb of sugar. How many 1 kg bags of sugar does Sarah need to buy so that she can make the cake?

....

Angle Rules

Hope you've learnt the rules for angles <u>in a triangle</u>, on a <u>straight line</u> and <u>round a point</u>. If not, you won't get far with these questions matey...

Q1   Work out the angles labelled:

c = ...

a = ...

b = ...

d = ...

e = ...

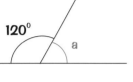

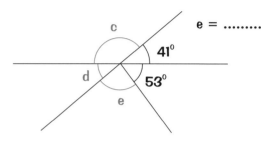

Q2   Work out the missing angle in each of these triangles.
The angles are not drawn to scale so you cannot measure them.

a) ....

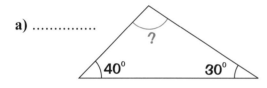

b) ....

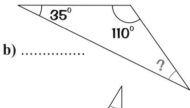

c) ....

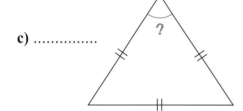

d) ....

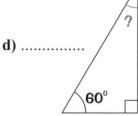

Q3   **a)** Calculate angle b.

....

b) Find angle a.

....

c) Calculate angle e.

....

d) Which angle is equal to angle e?

....

e) Calculate angle c.

....

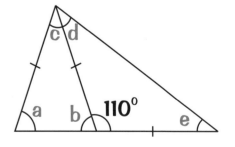

Find the isosceles triangles in the diagram and think what this tells you about their angles.

Coordinates

Remember — 1) **X comes before Y**

2) **X goes a-cross (get it) the page.** (Ah, the old ones are the best...)

Q1 The map shows the island of Tenerife where the sun never stops shining...

a) Use the map to write down the coordinates of the following:

Airport (.... , ...)

Mount Teide (.... , ...)

Santa Cruz (.... , ...)

Puerto Colon (.... , ...)

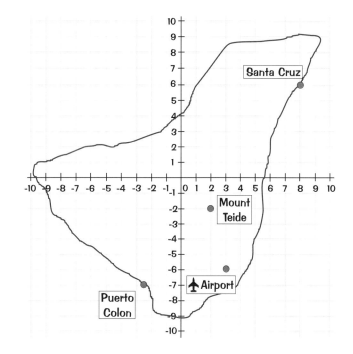

b) Use the coordinates given to mark the following holiday destinations on the map.

Las Americas (-4 , -6), El Medano (4 , -4), Icod (-6 , 2), Laguna (3 , 7), Taganana (9 , 9)

c) The cable car takes you to the top of Mount Teide. It starts at (3 , 1) and ends at (2 , -2). Draw the cable car route on the map.

Q2 On the graph paper below, draw the following lines:

a) $y = -2$

b) $x = -4$

c) $y = 1.5$

d) $x = 2.5$

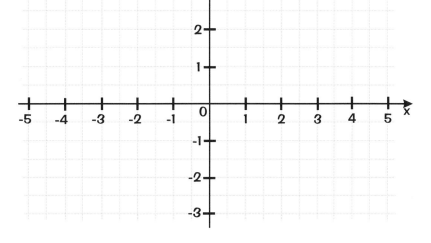

Reflection and Rotational Symmetry

Nothing too bad here — reflection's just mirror drawing really. Then, "order of rotational symmetry" is just a fancy way of saying how many <u>positions</u> look the same.

Q1 a) Reflect each shape in the line x = 4.

b) Write down the coordinates of A.

(........., ...)

c) Write down the new coordinates of A after the reflection.

(........., ...)

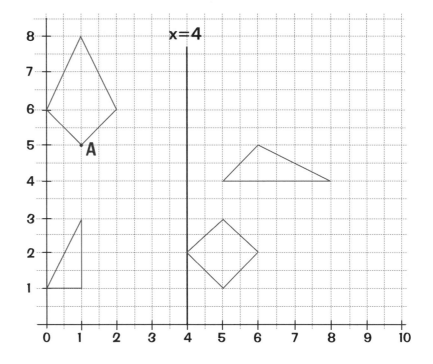

Q2 Write down the order of rotational symmetry of each of the following shapes:

a)

square

....

b)

rectangle

....

c)

equilateral triangle

....

d)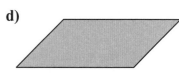

parallelogram

....

Q3 Complete the following diagrams so that they have rotational symmetry about centre C of the order stated:

a)   order 2

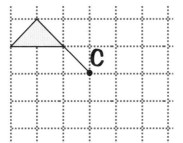

b)   order 4

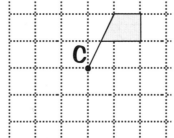

c)   order 3

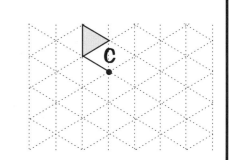

Probability

 There are two types of probability questions you need to be sure you can do. __Calculating probabilities__ — where you look at the number of outcomes that give the event. And __estimating probabilities__ — where you look at the number of times the event has happened.

Q1 Write down, as a fraction, the probability of these events happening:

a) Throwing a 5 with an unbiased six-sided dice. ....

b) Drawing a red card from a pack of cards. ....

c) Drawing a king from a pack of cards. ....

d) Throwing a 0 with a dice. ....

Q2 One letter is chosen from the word '**MILITARY**'. What is the probability that the letter is:

a) an R? ....

b) an I? ....

c) a vowel? ....

All you need to know for part a) is how many Rs there are and how many letters altogether.

Q3 The number of pets owned by ten people are shown below.

$$2, 0, 0, 1, 4, 5, 3, 6, 1, 0$$

One of the people is chosen at random. Calculate the probability that they own:

a) 2 pets ....

b) more than 3 pets ....

Q4 Joe has a 4-sided spinner, with sides numbered 1 to 4.
He spins the spinner 100 times, and gets the following results:

Score	1	2	3	4
Frequency	18	20	40	22

Estimate the probability of getting a '2' with Joe's spinner. ....

Q5 Carla wants to estimate the league position her local dominos team will finish in this year. This graph shows the number of times they have finished in each position over the last 50 years:

a) Estimate the probabilities of the team finishing in each of the six positions this year.

1st: ...., 2nd: ...., 3rd: ...., 4th: ...., 5th: ...., 6th: ....

b) What position is the team most likely to finish in this year? Explain your answer.

.... , because ....

Averages

Geesh — as if it's not enough to make you work out all these boring averages, they want you to write stuff about them as well. Oh well, here goes nothing.

Q1   Here is a set of data: 5, 2, 3, 2, 9, 4, 2, 5

    a) Calculate the mean for the data ....

    b) Calculate the median for the data ....

    c) Write down the mode for the data ....

    d) Work out the range of the data ....

Q2   The number of absences for 20 pupils during the spring term were:

        0 0 0 0 0 0 1 1 1 2 3 4 4 4 7 9 10 10 19 22

    a) Work out the mean, median and modal number of absences.

        ....

        ....

    b) If you were a local newspaper reporter wishing to show that the local school has a very poor attendance record, which average would you use and why?

        ....

    c) If you were the headteacher writing a report for the parents of new pupils, which average would you use and why?

        ....

Q3   The shoe sizes in a class of girls are:

        3 3 4 4 5 5 5 5 6 6 6 7 8

    a) Calculate the mean, median and mode for the shoe sizes.

        ....

        ....

    b) If you were a shoe shop manager, which average would be most useful to you, and why?

        ....

Think about what each of the averages is actually telling you.

Rounding and Estimating

Q1   Round the following to the nearest whole number:

   a) 2.9 ....   **b)** 26.8 ....   **c)** 2.24 ....

   d) 11.11 ....   **e)** 6.347 ....   **f)** 43.5 ....

   g) 9.99 ....   **h)** 0.41 ....

> Nearest <u>whole number</u> means you look at the digit after the decimal point to decide whether to round up or down.

Q2   By the time she is 25 the average woman will have driven 4.72 cars. What is this to the nearest whole number?

   ....

Q3   Round off these numbers to the nearest 10:

   a) 23 ....   **b)** 65 ....   **c)** 118 ....   **d)** 958 ....

Q4   Round off these numbers to the nearest 100:

   a) 627 ....   **b)** 199 ....   **c)** 1288 ....   **d)** 2993 ....

Q5   Crowd sizes at sports events are often given exactly in newspapers. Round off these exact crowd sizes to the nearest 1000:

   a) 23324 ....   **b)** 36844 ....   **c)** 49752 ....

Q6   Round off these numbers to 1 decimal place (1 d.p.):

   a) 7.34 ....   **b)** 8.47 ....   **c)** 12.08 ....   **d)** 28.03 ....

   e) 9.35 ....   **f)** 14.618 ....   **g)** 30.409 ....   **h)** 42.55 ....

Q7   Round off the following to 2 d.p.:

   a) 17.363 ....   **b)** 38.057 ....   **c)** 0.735 ....

Q8   Dom invites some friends round for a barbeque. All the food for the barbeque comes to £60. They decide to share the cost equally between them. If there are 7 people including Dom, how much should they each pay? Round the answer to the nearest penny.

   ....

Rounding and Estimating

Q9 Round these numbers to 1 significant figure.

a) 12 .... **b)** 530 ....

The 1st significant figure of any number is the first digit which isn't zero.

c) 1379 .... **d)** 0.021 ....

e) 1829.62 .... **f)** 0.296 ....

Q10 At a golf club, a putting green is given as being 500 cm long to 1 significant figure. Give the range of values that the actual length of the green could be.

....

To estimate a calculation, just round off to NICE EASY NUMBERS, then use them to do the sum. Easy peasy.

Q11 Estimate the answers to these questions…

For example: 12 × 21 <u>10 × 20 = 200</u>

a) 18 × 12 .... × .... = ... **b)** 545 × 301 .... × .... = ...

c) 901 ÷ 33 .... ÷ .... = ... **d)** 1207 ÷ 598 .... ÷ .... = ...

Q12 Write in the estimates that give the answer shown.

For example: 101 × 96 <u>100 × 100 = 10000</u>

a) 67 × 89 .... × .... = 6300 **b)** 99 × 9 .... × .... = 1000

c) 182 ÷ 62 .... ÷ .... = 3 **d)** 317 ÷ 81 .... ÷ .... = 4

Q13 Andy earns £12,404 a year. Bob earns £58,975 a year. Chris earns £81,006 a year.

a) Estimate how much Andy will earn over 3 years. £ ....

b) Estimate how many years Andy will have to work to earn as much as Chris does in one year. ....

c) Estimate how much Bob earns per month. £ ....

Cube Numbers and Negative Numbers

Cube numbers are a doddle if you just remember this simple example...

"Six cubed" written in <u>index notation</u> is 6^3 which means $6 \times 6 \times 6$.
$6 \times 6 \times 6 = 216$, so 216 is called a "cube number".

No calculators for this page.

Q1 Find the first 6 cube numbers.

$1 \times 1 \times 1 =$ .... , $2 \times 2 \times 2 =$ .... , ... ,

.... , ... , ...

Q2 What is the cube of these numbers?

a) 2 .... **b)** 10 .... **c)** 20 ....

Q3 Find the value of these:

Index notation is just a quick way of writing something multiplied lots of times. E.g. 4^6 is $4 \times 4 \times 4 \times 4 \times 4 \times 4$

a) $3^2 =$ .... **d)** $9^2 =$ ....

b) $1^5 =$ .... **e)** $2^4 =$ ....

c) $2^3 =$ .... **f)** $7^3 =$ ....

Q4 Write these in index notation.

a) $2 \times 2 \times 2 \times 2 =$ .... **c)** $6 \times 6 \times 6 =$ ....

b) $3 \times 3 \times 3 \times 3 =$ .... **d)** $5 \times 5 \times 5 \times 5 \times 5 =$ ....

Time for some practice with negative number calculations. For adding and subtracting, always <u>draw a number line</u> so you can see what's going on. No calculators, remember.

Q5 Work out:

a) $-2 + 5 =$ .... **c)** $-6 + 10 =$ .... **e)** $-2 + 50 =$ ....

b) $-3 - 2 =$ .... **d)** $-3 - 6 =$ .... **f)** $-13 - 3 =$ ....

Q6 Work out:

a) $-4 \times -3 =$ .... **d)** $-8 \div 4 =$ ....

b) $5 \times -2 =$ .... **e)** $-20 \div -10 =$ ....

c) $-12 \div -4 =$ .... **f)** $2 \times -3 \times -2 =$ ....

Rules for Multiplying and Dividing		
$\times$ or $\div$	$+$ve	$-$ve
$+$ ve	$+$	$-$
$-$ ve	$-$	$+$

OCR MODULAR MATHS — MODULE 5

Fractions

To make an **EQUIVALENT** fraction, you've got to multiply or divide the **TOP** (numerator) and **BOTTOM** (denominator) by the <u>same thing</u>.

No calculators for the first five questions....

Q1   Write in the missing numbers to make these fractions equivalent. E.g. 1/2 = 7/14

   a) 1/4 = 4/......   **b)** 3/4 = 9/......   **c)** 1/3 = .../6

   d) 2/3 = 8/......   **e)** 2/7 = 6/......   **f)** 6/18 = 1/......

Q2   Write in the missing numbers to make each list equivalent.

   a) 1/2 = 2/...... = .../6 = .../8 = 5/10 = 25/...... = .../70 = .../100

   b) 200/300 = 100/...... = .../15 = 40/...... = 120/180 = .../9 = .../3

Q3   Cancel down these fractions to express them in their simplest form.

   a) 8/16 = ...   **b)** 24/32 = ...

   c) 57/60 = ...   **d)** 45/72 = ...

   e) 14/21 = ...   **f)** 150/600 = ...

Q4   What fraction of 1 hour is: **Q5**   If a TV programme lasts 40 minutes, what fraction of the programme is left after:

   a) 5 minutes? ....

   b) 15 minutes? ....   **a)** 10 minutes? ....

   c) 40 minutes? ....   **b)** 15 minutes? ....

   c) 35 minutes? ....

OK, you can use your calculator now...

Q6   Express each of the following as a percentage. Round off if necessary.

   a) £8 of £12 = ...   **b)** £7 of £16 = ...

   c) 600 kg of 750 kg = ...   **d)** 6 hours of one day = ...

   e) 1 month of a year = ...   **f)** 25 m of 65 m = ...

Q7   There were 65 people at a jungle-themed party. 20% came dressed as Declan Donnelly, 2/5 came dressed as Ant McPartlin. Everyone else came dressed as Ant-eaters. How many people came as Ant-eaters?

....

Percentages

Finding "something %" of "something-else" is really quite simple —
so you'd better be sure you know how...

E.g. 30% of 150 would be $\frac{30}{100} \times 150 = 45$

Q1   A school has 750 pupils.

a) If 56% of the pupils are boys, what percentage are girls? ....

b) How many boys are there in the school? ....

c) One day, 6% of the pupils were absent. How many pupils was this? ....

d) 54% of the pupils have a school lunch, 38% bring sandwiches and the rest go home for
lunch. How many pupils go home for lunch?

....

Q2   VAT (value added tax) is
charged at a rate of 17.5%
on many goods and services.
Complete the table showing
how much VAT has to be
paid and the new price.

Article	Basic price	VAT at 17.5%	Price + VAT
Tin of paint	£6.75		
Paint brush	£3.60		
Sand paper	£1.55		

Q3   Admission to Wonder World is £18 for adults. A child ticket is 60% of the adult price.

a) How much will it cost for one adult and 4 children to enter Wonder World?

....

b) How much will two adults and three children spend on entrance tickets?

....

Q4   Terence paid £4700 for his new motorcycle. Each year its value decreased by 12%.

a) How much was it worth when it was one year old?   ....

b) How much was it worth when it was two years old?   ....

Q5 a) Mani books a jungle-trekking holiday to Peru. The price is £1500 plus a 5% fee
to cover insurance and booking costs. How much will Mani have to pay?

....

b) Sam books a jungle-trekking holiday to Blackpool. The normal cost if £59,
but it currently has a 35% discount. How much will Sam have to pay?

....

Expressions — Simplifying and Substitution

The secret to algebra is just to **practise** lots of questions. Eventually you'll be able to do it without thinking, just like riding a bike. But a lot more fun, obviously...

Q1 By collecting like terms, simplify the following. The first one is done for you.

a) $6x + 3x - 5 = 9x - 5$

e) $3x + 4y + 12x - 5y = $ ....

b) $2x + 3x - 5x = $ ....

f) $11a + 6b + 24a + 18b = $ ....

c) $9f + 16f + 15 - 30 = $ ....

g) $9f + 16g - 15f - 30g = $ ....

d) $14x + 12x - 1 + 2x = $ ....

h) $14a + 12a^2 - 3 + 2a = $ ....

Q2 Write down and simplify an expression for the perimeter of this triangle:

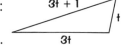

....

Q3 The ages of four friends are: x, x + 1, x + 2 and 2x.

a) Write down an expression for the total age of the friends. ....

b) Simplify your expression by collecting like terms. ....

Q4 a) Write down, as simply as possible, an expression for the total length of this squiggle:

....

b) Find the value of your expression when x = 2 and y = 3. ....

Q5 Below is a map of one of Father Christmas' present-delivery routes. He has marked on the number of presents he needs to deliver along the way.

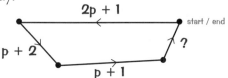

a) He plans to deliver 7p + 5 presents altogether. Write down, as simply as possible, an expression for the missing number of presents.

....

b) If p = 8, find the total number of presents Father Christmas delivers along this route.

....

See page 12 for more practice at substituting into formulas.

Solving Equations

You've got to get the letter on its own (e.g. x = ...).
You can add, divide... well, anything really — but you
gotta <u>do the same to both sides</u> or it'll all go horribly wrong.

Q1   Solve the following equations:

a) $4x = 20$

....

b) $7y = 28$

....

c) $7x = -14$

....

d) $2z = -18$

....

e) $100 = 10x$

....

f) $\dfrac{x}{2} = 22$

....

g) $\dfrac{x}{7} = 3$

....

h) $8 = \dfrac{a}{5}$

....

i) $x + 3 = 11$

....

j) $23 = x + 19$

....

k) $x - 6 = 13$

....

l) $-3 = x + 5$

....

m) $2x + 1 = 7$

....

n) $2x + 4 = 5$

....

o) $54 = 7x + 5$

....

p) $6y - 7 = 41$

....

q) $13 = 2x + 7$

....

r) $3x - 2 = 19$

....

Drawing Graphs from Tables

Always check your graph is a dead straight line. If it's not, you need to work out the offending y-value again and check you've plotted it correctly.

Q1 On the grid shown, draw axes with x from 0 to 8 and y from 0 to 14.

Q2 a) Complete the table of values for y = x + 2.

x	0	1	2	3	4	5	6
y	2			5			

b) Use your table of values to draw the graph of y = x + 2 on the grid opposite.

Q3 a) Complete the table below for y = 2x + 1

x	0	1	2	3	4	5	6
y	1				9		

b) Use your table of values to draw the graph of y = 2x + 1 on the grid opposite.

Q4 a) Fill in the table for y = 8 − x, using values of x from 0 to 6.

x							
y							

b) Draw the graph of y = 8 − x on the grid above.

That's it, I've had enough of those penguins — sticking their skinny beaks in where they're not wanted... squinting at you with those beady eyes... leaving eyebrow feathers here, there and everywhere. But I tell you — toucan play at their game. So expect to see less of them and more of me from now on.

Digital readers can access all previous penguin footage by pressing their red buttons now. Otherwise, view it by flicking to the following pages: 2, 6, 8, 9, 33, 41, 42, 43.

Drawing Triangles

Constructions need to be done as accurately as possible using a <u>sharp pencil</u>, <u>ruler</u> and <u>pair of compasses</u> or a <u>protractor</u>. Whether you use compasses or a protractor depends on what information you're given.

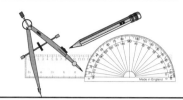

Q1 Make an accurate drawing below of this triangle. Measure side AB on your triangle, giving your answer in millimetres.

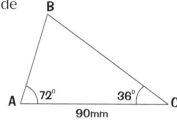

AB = ... mm

Q2 In the space to the right, construct a triangle ABC with AB = 6 cm, AC = 4 cm, BC = 3 cm. Measure angle C, giving your answer to the nearest degree.

Q3 Draw below an accurate full-size version of the triangle on the right. Measure side PQ on your triangle giving your answer in millimetres.

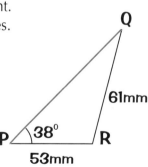

PQ = ... mm

62

Maps and Bearings

Bearings always have three digits — even the small ones...
in other words, if you've measured 60°, you've got to write it as 060°.

Q1 **a)** Estimate these bearings by eye.
b) Use a protractor or angle measurer to check your answers.

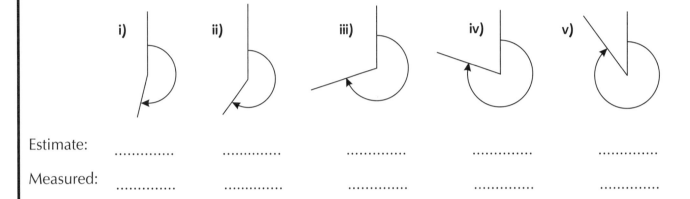

Estimate: ....

Measured: ....

Q2 This is a map of part of a coastline. The scale is one cm to one km.

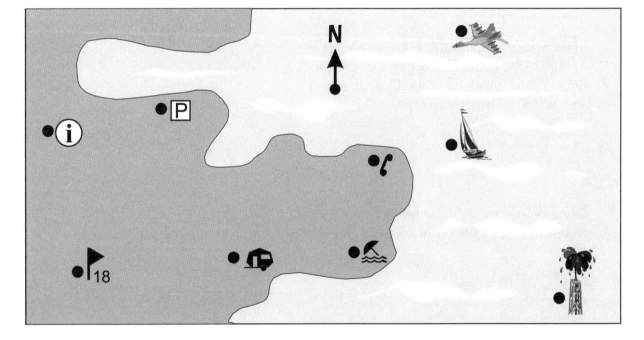

a) What is the bearing of the 🚐 from the ℹ️? ....

b) What is the bearing of the P from the 🏖️? ....

c) How far and on what bearing is:

   i) The boat from the plane? ....

   ii) The boat from the oil rig? ....

   iii) The plane from the oil rig? ....

Maps and Bearings

Q3 This is a map of the Channel Islands.

a) Which island is furthest West?

....

b) Which island is due East of Guernsey?

....

The dots show the airports. The grid reference of Jersey Airport is 3817.

c) Write down the grid references for:

Guernsey airport ....

Alderney airport ....

Sark airport ....

d) What bearing is needed to fly from Jersey to Guernsey? How far is it?

....

The flight from Jersey to Alderney goes directly over Sark.

e) What is the bearing for the first leg of the journey?

....

f) What is the bearing for the second leg of the journey?

....

g) Estimate the total distance flown from Jersey to Alderney.

....

h) Estimate the area of each of the islands, to the nearest 25 square miles.

Jersey ....

Guernsey ....

Alderney ....

Sark ....

You need to look at the scale to work out distances.

Start by working out what an area of 25 square miles looks like on the map.

Quadrilaterals

Here's a few easy marks for you — all you've got
to do is remember the shapes and a few facts
about them... it's a waste of marks not to bother.

Fill in the blanks in the table.

NAME	DRAWING	DESCRIPTION
Square		Sides of equal length. Opposite sides parallel. Four right angles.
....	....	Opposite sides parallel and the same length. Four right angles.
....		Opposite sides are .... and equal. Opposite angles are equal.
Trapezium		Only .... sides are parallel.
Rhombus		A parallelogram but with all sides ....
Kite	....	Two pairs of adjacent equal sides.

Cubes and Cuboids

This looks a bit familiar... one tricky shape made up of a few easier shapes.
(You know what to do with this — individual volumes first, then add together)

Q1   Calculate the volume of these podiums...

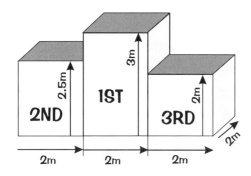

a) 1st Place = length × width × height

= ..... × ...... × ...... = ...m³

b) 2nd Place = ... × ..... × ..... = ...m³

c) 3rd Place = ... × ..... × ..... = ...m³

Total = ... + ... + ... = ...m³

Q2   How much water would this tank hold when full to the brim?

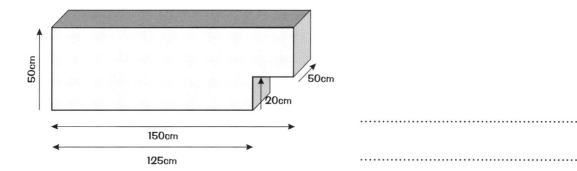

....

....

Q3   Which one of these is a
correct net of a cuboid?

....

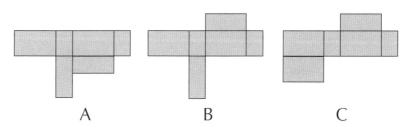

A   B   C

Q4   What is the volume of a cube of side:

a) 5 cm? ....

b) 9 cm? ....

c) 15 cm? ....

Rotation and Translation

A <u>½ turn clockwise</u> is the same as a <u>½ turn anti-clockwise</u> — and
a <u>¼ turn clockwise</u> is the same as a <u>¾ turn anti-clockwise</u>. Great fun, innit...

Q1 The centre of rotation for each of these diagrams is **X**. Rotate (turn) each shape as asked then draw the new position of the shape onto each of the diagrams below.

a) 180° (or ½ turn).

b) 270° anticlockwise (or ¾ turn anticlockwise).

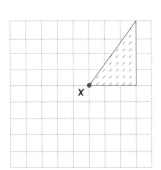 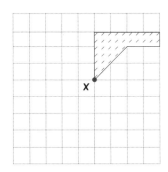

Q2 Rotate triangle PQR 90° anticlockwise about the origin 0.
Label the new triangle P'Q'R'.

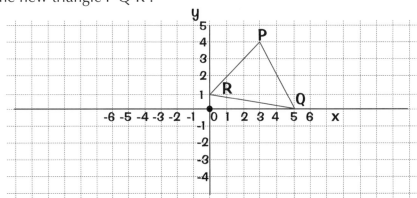

Q3 Translation is the sliding of a shape in a straight line from one position to another.
Do the following translations, labelling the images A', B' and C'.

A   4 left , 3 down   B   5 right, 5 up   C 4 right, 4 down

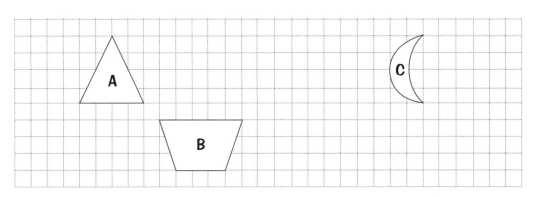

Probability

Remember — the probability of something not happening is just
1 minus the probability of it happening. Got that? Splendid.

Q1   If the probability of picking a banana from a fruit bowl is 0.27, what
is the probability of picking some other fruit which is not a banana?

....

Q2   Each time Syed makes toast, the probability he burns it is $\frac{1}{4}$.
Write down the probability that he doesn't burn his toast.

....

Q3   A bag contains 3 red balls, 4 blue balls and 5 green balls. A ball is chosen at random
from the bag. Find the probability that:

a) it is green ....   **c)** it is red ....

b) it is blue ....   **d)** it is not red ....

Q4   The outcome when a coin is tossed is head (H) or tail (T).
Complete this table of outcomes when two coins are tossed together.

a) How many possible outcomes are there? ....

b) What is the probability of getting 2 heads? ....

c) What is the probability of getting a head
followed by a tail? ....

		2nd COIN	
		H	**T**
1st COIN	**H**		
	T		

Q5   Two dice are rolled together. The scores on the dice are added.
Complete the table of possible outcomes below.

How many different combinations are there? ....

E.g. count (1,2) and (2,1) as
being different combinations.

What is the probability of scoring:

a) 2 ....

b) 6 ....

c) 10 ....

d) More than 9 ....

e) Less than 4 ....

f) An even number ....

g) An odd number? ....

SECOND DICE						
	1	**2**	**3**	**4**	**5**	**6**
1						
2	3					
3						
4						
5			8			
6						

FIRST DICE

Averages

Q1 These are some mathematics test marks for John and Mark.

John	65	83	58	79	75
Mark	72	70	81	67	70

a) Calculate the mean and range for each pupil.

....

b) Who do you think is the better maths student? Why?

....

Q2 The bar graph shows the amount of time Jim and Bob spend watching TV during the week.

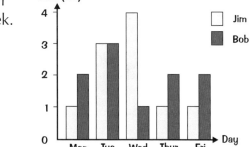

a) Find the mean amount of time per day each spends watching TV.

....

....

b) Find the range of times for each of them.

....

c) Using your answers from **a)** and **b)**, comment on what you notice about the way they watch TV.

....

Q3 The Borders Orchid Growers Society has measured the heights of all the Lesser Plumed Bog Orchids in the 5 miles wide strip each side of the border, to the nearest cm.

5 miles on Scottish side
Heights 14, 15, 17, 14, 17, 16, 14, 13
15, 17, 16, 14, 15, 17, 14, 13

5 miles on English side
Heights 14, 12, 16, 18, 19, 17, 16, 15
13, 14, 15, 16, 17, 18, 19, 13

a) State the mode and median for each set of data.

....

b) Find the range for each set of data.

....

c) On which side of the border are you likely to see taller Orchids? Explain your answer.

....

d) On which side of the border are the orchids more of a standard size? Explain your answer.

....

Pie Charts

Q1 In a University department there are 180 students from different countries.

Country	UK	Malaysia	Spain	Others
Number of students	90	35	10	45

To show this on a Pie chart you have to work out the angle of each sector. Complete the table showing your working. The UK is done for you.

COUNTRY	WORKING	ANGLE in degrees
UK	90 ÷ 180 × 360 =	180°
MALAYSIA		
SPAIN		
OTHERS		

Now complete the Pie chart using an angle measurer. The UK sector is done for you.

Q2 The table shows the daily amount of air time of programme types on a TV channel. Complete the table by calculating the pie chart angle for each programme type.

Programme	Hours	Angle
News	5	
Sport	3	
Music	2	
Current Affairs	3	
Comedy	2	
Other	9	
Total	24	

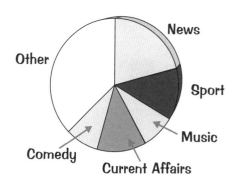

Q3 In a survey, 120 people tried 5 different flavours of a new range of smoothie drinks and were asked to choose their favourite. The pie chart shows the results.

a) How many people liked orange and beetroot best?

....

b) What fraction of the pie chart shows those who preferred peppermint, peach and parsnip?

....

c) How many people altogether chose mango and cabbage or apple and sprout?

....

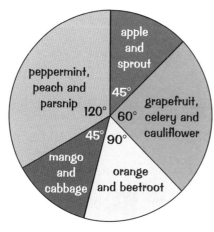

d) How many people preferred grapefruit, celery and cauliflower?

....

MODULE 6

Calculator Questions

Yeah, OK, we all know how to do sums on a calculator — but it can do so much more... check out the groovy powers button and the funky brackets buttons, not to mention the slinky **1/x** button...

Q1 Using the **x²** button on your calculator, work out:

a) 1^2 .... **c)** 16^2 .... **e)** $(-5)^2$ ....

b) 2^2 .... **d** $(-1)^2$ .... **f)** 1000^2 ....

Q2 Using the **xʸ** or **∧** button, find:

a) 1^3 .... **c)** 4^5 .... **e)** 2^{-1} ....

b) 3^6 .... **d)** 3^{-2} .... **f)** 0^2 ....

Q3 Using the reciprocal button **1/x** on your calculator, work out:

a) $\dfrac{1}{3^3}$ .... **b)** $\dfrac{1}{4^{-2}}$ .... **c)** $\dfrac{1}{1+3^2-4^2}$ ....

Q4 Using the **√** button on your calculator, work out:

a) $\sqrt{16}$ .... **d)** $\sqrt{0}$ .... **g)** $\sqrt{3}$ ....

b) $\sqrt{36}$ .... **e)** $\sqrt{3600}$ .... **h)** $\sqrt{7}$ ....

c) $\sqrt{289}$ .... **f)** $\sqrt{400}$ .... **i)** $\sqrt{30}$ ....

Q5 Using **(** and **)** , calculate:

a) $\dfrac{(14+18)}{(2\times8)}$ .... **b)** $\dfrac{(9+(4\div2))}{(11\times3)}$ .... **c)** $\dfrac{12}{(8+9)(13-11)}$ ....

Q6 Use your calculator to work out:

a) the cost of 5 sherbet beetles for 56p each and 10 fizzy slugs for £1.21 each. ....

b) the cost to the nearest penny of 1 cola emu if a pack of 36 costs £2.49. ....

Q7 Use the **°'"** button to do these time conversions:

E.g. to enter 3 hrs 23 mins 5 sec into your calculator, you'd press:
3 **°'"** **23** **°'"** **5** **°'"** **=**

a) 1 hour 23 min 30 s into hours ....

b) 1.355 hrs into "hours, minutes and seconds" ....

Ratio

Ratios compare quantities of the same kind — so if the units aren't mentioned, they've got to be the same in each bit of the ratio.

Q1 Write each of these ratios in its simplest form. The first one is done for you.

a) 4 to 6

2 : 3

b) 15 to 21

...... : ......

c) 14 to 42

.... : ......

d) 72 to 45

.... : ......

e) 24 cm to 36 cm

...... : ......

f) 350 g to 2 kg

...... : ......

g) 42p to £1.36

...... : ......

Watch out for ones like f) and g) — you need to make the units the same first.

Q2 The ratio of men to women at a football match was 11:4.
How many men were there if there were:

a) 2000 women? ....

b) 8460 women? ....

How many women were there if there were:

c) 22000 men? ....

d) 6820 men? ....

Q3 A recipe for Ozzy's Speciality Omelette serves 4 people and uses 3/4 pint of herbal tea.
How much herbal tea will be needed to make an omelette for:

a) 32 people? ....

b) 96 people? ....

Q4 Ozzy's Speciality Orange Smoothie is made by mixing orange juice and herbal tea in the ratio 7 : 1.

a) How much orange juice is needed to make 600 ml of smoothie? ....

b) How many ml of tea are needed to make 1 litre of smoothie? ....

c) If 200 ml of tea are used, how much smoothie will be made? ....

Decimal Arithmetic

 Time to test your <u>written methods</u> for adding, subtracting, multiplying and dividing. But if you want to practise some easier questions first, have a look back at <u>p4-6</u> and <u>p35-37</u>.

<u>NO CALCULATORS</u> for any of these questions...

Q1   Work out these additions and subtractions:

a)   2.4
    +3.2

b)   14.82
    +23.02

c)   86.05
    − 72.95

d)   7.34
    + 6.07

e)   9.93
    − 3.38

Q2   Now try these multiplications.

Count the number of d.p.s in the question and put the same number into your answer.

a) 6.2 × 4

b) 8.6 × 5

c) 4.75 × 3

= ....

= ....

= ....

d) 66.2 × 0.2

e) 263 × 1.4

f) 2.52 × 0.13

= ....

= ....

= ....

Q3   Have a go at these divisions now.

a) 27.2 ÷ 4

b) 31.8 ÷ 6

c) 52.15 ÷ 7

d) 91.2 ÷ 2.4

e) 2.6 ÷ 0.4

f) 3.6 ÷ 0.4

Q4   Finally, use division to convert these fractions to decimals:

a) $\frac{3}{5}$

b) $\frac{2}{3}$

c) $\frac{3}{8}$

d) $\frac{5}{8}$

e) $\frac{5}{16}$

Fraction Arithmetic

Fraction arithmetic becomes a nice stroll in the desert, once you've <u>learned the rules</u>:

<u>MULTIPLYING</u> — multiply top and bottom separately,
<u>DIVIDING</u> — invert the second fraction then treat like multiplication.
<u>ADDING</u> / <u>SUBTRACTING</u> — put over a common denominator,
then add / subtract the top line only.

No calculators for any of these questions...

Q1 Change these top-heavy fractions to mixed numbers:

a) $\frac{3}{2}$ = ... b) $\frac{7}{4}$ = ... c) $\frac{8}{3}$ = ...

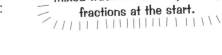
For some of the questions below, you'll need to change the mixed fractions into top-heavy fractions at the start.

Change these mixed numbers to top-heavy fractions:

d) $2\frac{1}{2}$ = ... e) $3\frac{1}{3}$ = ... f) $1\frac{3}{5}$ = ...

Q2 Do these multiplications, giving the answers as fractions in their lowest terms:

a) $\frac{4}{3}\times\frac{3}{4}$ .... d) $2\frac{1}{2}\times\frac{3}{5}$ ....

b) $\frac{2}{5}\times\frac{3}{4}$ .... e) $10\frac{2}{7}\times\frac{7}{9}$ ....

c) $\frac{11}{9}\times\frac{6}{5}$ .... f) $2\frac{1}{6}\times3\frac{1}{3}$ ....

For more fraction practice, I'd thoroughly recommend a look back at p38.

Q3 Now do these divisions, giving the answers in their lowest terms:

a) $\frac{1}{4}\div\frac{3}{8}$ .... d) $1\frac{1}{2}\div\frac{5}{12}$ ....

b) $\frac{1}{9}\div\frac{2}{3}$ .... e) $10\frac{4}{5}\div\frac{9}{10}$ ....

c) $\frac{15}{24}\div\frac{6}{5}$ .... f) $3\frac{7}{11}\div1\frac{4}{11}$ ....

Q4 Add the two fractions, giving your answer as a fraction in its lowest terms:

a) $\frac{7}{8}+\frac{3}{8}$ .... b) $\frac{1}{12}+\frac{3}{4}$ .... c) $\frac{1}{3}+\frac{3}{4}$ ....

d) $1\frac{2}{5}+2\frac{2}{3}$ .... e) $\frac{1}{6}+4\frac{1}{3}$ .... f) $1\frac{3}{10}+\frac{2}{5}$ ....

Q5 Evaluate, giving your answer as a fraction in its lowest terms:

a) $\frac{11}{4}-\frac{2}{3}$ .... b) $10-\frac{2}{5}$ .... c) $1\frac{3}{4}-1\frac{1}{5}$ ....

d) $4\frac{2}{3}-\frac{7}{9}$ .... e) $3\frac{1}{2}-\frac{2}{3}$ .... f) $8-\frac{1}{8}$ ....

Q6 By finding the common denominator, put these fractions in order of size, smallest first.

$\frac{2}{5}$ $\frac{2}{3}$ $\frac{1}{2}$ $\frac{7}{10}$ $\frac{8}{15}$ ....

Algebra

With night comes day, with dark comes light, and with <u>multiplying out brackets</u> comes <u>putting them back in again...</u>

Q1 Multiply out the brackets and then simplify if possible. The first one is done for you.

Careful with the minus signs — they multiply both terms in the bracket.

a) $2(x + y) = 2x + 2y$

e) $-(y - 2) =$ ....

b) $4(x - 3) =$ ....

f) $x(y + 2) =$ ....

c) $8(x^2 + 2) =$ ....

g) $x(x + y + z) =$ ....

d) $-2(x + 5) =$ ....

h) $8(a + b) + 2(a + 2b) =$ ....

Q2 Factorise the expressions below. Each has 4 as a common factor.

a) $4x + 8 =$ ....

c) $4 - 16x =$ ....

b) $12 - 8x =$ ....

d) $4x^2 + 64 =$ ....

Q3 Factorise the expressions below.

a) $21 - 7x =$ ....

c) $14 + 21x =$ ....

b) $28x + 7 =$ ....

d) $35x^2 - 14 =$ ....

Q4 Factorise the expressions below.

a) $2x + x^2 =$ ....

d) $8y^2 - 5xy^2 =$ ....

b) $3a + 6b^2 =$ ....

e) $2t + 7t^2 =$ ....

c) $xyz - x^2 =$ ....

f) $pqr^2 + 2r =$ ....

Solving Equations and Substituting into Formulas

Q1 Solve these equations:

a) $3x + 2 = 14$

....

b) $\dfrac{8 + 6x}{5} = 10$

....

c) $5x - 4 = 31$

....

d) $-61 = 20 - 3x$

....

Q2 Now solve the following:

a) $3(2x + 1) = 27$

....

b) $5x + 3 = 2x + 15$

....

c) $3x + 5 = 2(4x - 10)$

....

d) $2(4x + 1) + x = 56$

....

e) $2(x + 7) = 6x - 10$

....

f) $-(x + 2) = 2(x + 2)$

....

Now for some practice at substituting into formulas.
Remember to use **BODMAS** to get the order of operations right.

Q3 If $x = 3$ and $y = 6$ find the value of the following expressions.

a) $x + 2y$ ....

b) $2x \div y$ ....

c) $2x^2$ ....

d) $2y^2$ ....

e) $x^2 + 5$ ....

f) $2x^3 - 3$ ....

Q4 Work out the value of $4y^2 + y^3$ when:

a) $y = 2$ ....

b) $y = -2$ ....

Q5 Using the formula $z = (x - 10)^2$, find the value of z when:

a) $x = 20$ ....

b) $x = -1$ ....

c) $x = -10$ ....

Q6 The volume of a sphere is found using the formula $\frac{4}{3}\pi r^3$, where r is the radius of the sphere. Find (to 1 d.p.) the volume of a sphere with a radius of:

a) 2 cm ....

b) 5 cm ....

Drawing Graphs from Equations

Before you get started here, have a go at the questions on <u>page 60</u>. For module 6, you might also get equations that need <u>rearranging</u> before you can draw the graph.

Q1 On the diagram:

    a) Draw and label the line y = x.

    b) Draw and label the line y = -x.

    c) Draw the line x = -3.

    d) Draw the line y = -2.

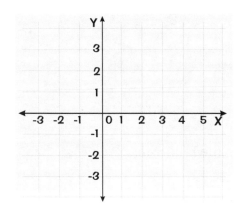

Q2 On the grid shown, draw axes with x from 0 to 8 and y from 0 to 14.

Q3 **a)** Complete the table of values for y – 1 = x, by first rearranging the equation.

    y = ...

x	0	1	2	3	4	5	6
y	1			4			

    b) Use your table of values to draw the graph of y – 1 = x on the grid opposite.

Q4 **a)** Complete the table below for y + x = 10.

x	0	1	2	3	4	5	6
y	10			6			

    b) Use your table of values to draw the graph of y + x = 10 on the grid opposite.

Q5 **a)** Fill in the table for y – 2x = 2, using values of x from 0 to 6.

x							
y							

    b) Draw the graph of y – 2x = 2 on the grid above.

When you've finished drawing graphs, have a go at <u>page 46</u> on interpreting graphs. You need to be able to do these types of questions for module 6 too.

Polygons

WARNING — do not attempt polygon questions without knowing the following formulas:

<u>Sum of Exterior angles = 360°</u> and <u>Sum of Interior angles = (n − 2) × 180°</u>

(where n is the number of sides)

Now with this knowledge, you'll be able to handle <u>polygons backwards</u>.

Q1 Here is a regular octagon:

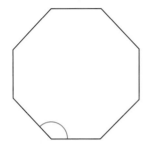

a) What is the total of its eight interior angles?

....

b) What is the size of the marked angle?

....

Here is a regular pentagon:

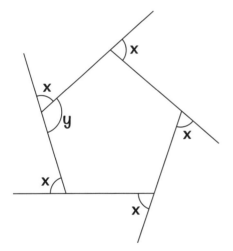

c) The five angles marked x are its exterior angles. What do they add up to?

....

d) Work out the value of x.

....

e) Use your answer from part **d)** to work out the value of angle y.

....

Q2 The diagram shows a regular hexagon:

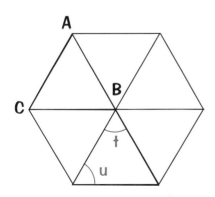

a) Work out the size of angles t and u.

....

b) What type of triangle is ABC? ....

I think the "joke" is polygons backwards ... snog ylop

I see... oh dear

Parallel Lines

Once you know the <u>three angle rules</u> for parallel lines, there's no end to the amount of angle fun you can have — you'll see what I mean...

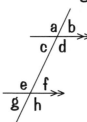

c = f and d = e — Alternate angles

a = e, c = g, b = f and d = h — Corresponding angles

d + f = 180°, c + e = 180° — Supplementary angles

Q1 Find the sizes of the angles marked by letters in these diagrams.
Write down what sort of angle each one is. *i.e. alternate, corresponding or supplementary*

NOT DRAWN TO SCALE

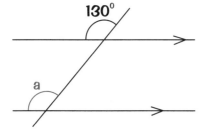

a = ...

b = ...

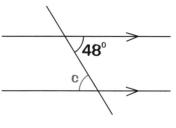

c = ...

d = ...

e = ...

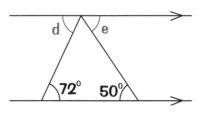

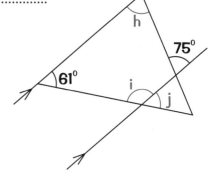

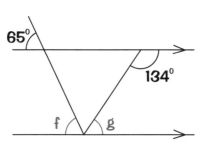

f = ...

g = ...

h = ...

i = ...

j = ...

Perimeter and Area

The 'big blob method' for finding perimeters is like an old friend — it never lets you down. Put a blob at one corner, then go round adding up the sides till you're back at the blob.

Q1 Work out the perimeters of the following shapes:

a) Symmetrical Five Sided Shape

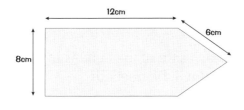

....

b) Symmetrical Four Sided Shape

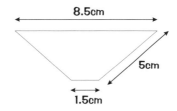

....

c)

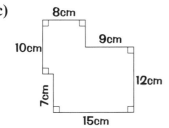

....

d)

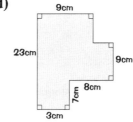

....

Q2 Calculate the areas of these composite shapes.

> Just add up the separate bits.

a)

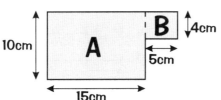

Shape A = ... cm²

Shape B = ... cm²

Total area = ... cm²

b) Area = ...

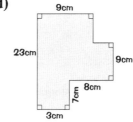

Q3 Find the shaded area in the diagram below.

> You have to think a bit more with this one, but you still only need to find the areas of two shapes.

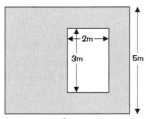

....

OCR Modular Maths — Module 6

80

Areas

Q1 A metal blade for a craft knife is the shape of a trapezium. Calculate the area of the metal.

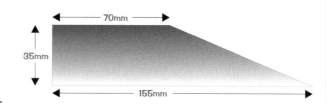

....

Q2 A cube bean bag is to be made out of material. If each side of the cube is to have edges of length 60 cm, how many square metres of material will be needed?

....

Q3 This parallelogram has an area of 4773 mm². How long is its base?

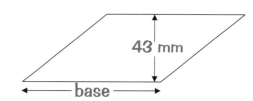

....

> Remember, a parallelogram is just a sloping rectangle — so area = base × vertical height.

Q4 A hanging basket bracket of sheet metal is stamped out in a 2 phase process:-

<u>1st</u>: The outer triangle, measuring 14.4 cm by 10 cm, is stamped out.
<u>2nd</u>: A smaller inner triangle measuring 5.76 cm by 4 cm is stamped out of the larger triangle.
How much metal makes up the finished bracket?

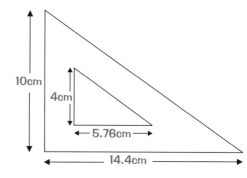

....

Q5 A lawn is to be made 48 m².
a) If its width is 5 m, how long is it?

....

b) Rolls of turf are 50 cm wide and 11 m long. How many rolls need to be ordered to grass the lawn?

....

> Start by finding the area of 1 roll. Then work out how many rolls fit into the area of the lawn.

....

The Circle Formulas

Don't worry about that π bit — it just stands for the number **3.14159...** Sometimes you'll be told to round it off to **3** or **3.14**. If not, just use the π button on your calculator.

Q1 Calculate the circumference of the circles below.
Take π to be 3.14, and give your answers to 3 sig. figs.

a) 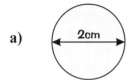 Circumference = π × diameter = ...

b) Circumference = ...

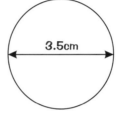

c)

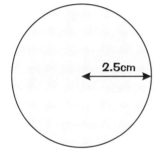

Remember to work out the diameter first.

Diameter = ...

Circumference = ...

d) A circle of radius 3.5 cm. ....

Q2 A coin has a diameter of 1.7 cm. What is its circumference? ....

Q3 Calculate the area of each circle. Give your answers to 3 sig. figs.

a)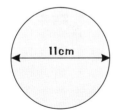

You must find the radius first.

Radius = ...

Area = ...

b) A circle of diameter 28 cm. Radius = ...

Area = ...

Q4 Calculate the area of the coin in question 2. ....

Solids and Nets

 A net is just a solid shape folded out flat. And what's more, <u>the area of the net is the surface area of the solid</u>. For more practice at solids and nets questions see <u>page 22</u>.

Q1 **a)** On a separate piece of paper, draw an accurate 2-dimensional net that would fold to make the 3-D cuboid shown.

b) Use your net to find the surface area of the cuboid.

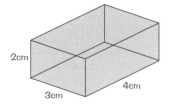

....

Q2 **a)** On a separate piece of paper, draw an accurate net for each of the following solids.

1)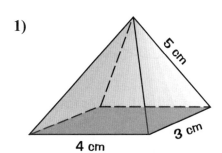

2)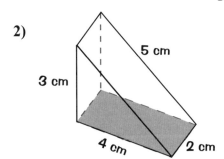

b) Using your net, find the surface area of shape **2)**.

....

Q3 Look at the shape opposite.

a) Draw the plan view and side elevation (looking from the right) in the space below.

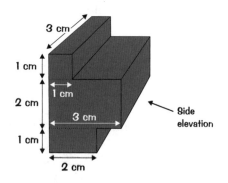

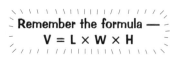
Remember the formula —
$$V = L \times W \times H$$

b) Calculate the volume of the shape.

....

Now look back at **page 65** for more practice at finding volumes of cuboids.

Drawing Shapes

Drawing shapes is the most like Art that Maths will ever be, so make the most of it.
If you'd like to do some more drawing shapes questions look back at pages 21 and 61.

Q1 Use a ruler and a protractor to construct the following:

a) an equilateral triangle with sides 5 cm

b) a square with sides 6 cm

Q2 Construct these polygons in the space below:

a) a regular pentagon

b) a regular octagon

Start these by drawing an accurate circle with a pair of compasses.

Transformations

Two whole pages of transformations for you here. And if that's not enough, you can find more on pages 27, 50 and 66.

Q1 a) Translate the shapes A, B and C using these vectors:
Label the images A′, B′ and C′.

$$A \begin{pmatrix} -2 \\ 4 \end{pmatrix} \quad B \begin{pmatrix} 3 \\ -4 \end{pmatrix} \quad C \begin{pmatrix} -1 \\ -2 \end{pmatrix}$$

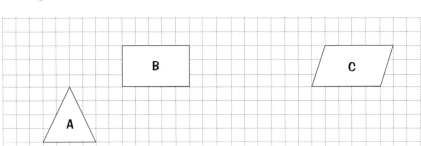

b) Write the translation vectors for: A′ → A ...., B′ → B ...., and C′ → C ....

Q2 a) Enlarge this triangle using scale factor 4 and centre of enlargement C.

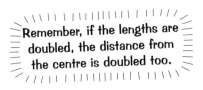

Remember, if the lengths are doubled, the distance from the centre is doubled too.

b) What can you say about the perimeter of the enlarged triangle compared to the original? ....

Q3 a) Enlarge this shape using scale factor 2 and centre of enlargement E.

b) Now enlarge the original shape using scale factor 0.5 and centre of enlargement F.

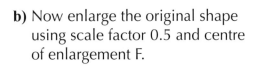

Careful — this is actually a reduction.

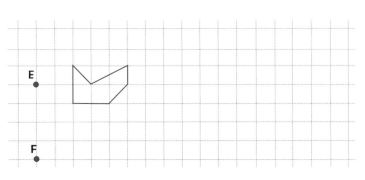

c) Are these three shapes congruent? Explain your answer.

....

Transformations

Q4   The centre of rotation for this diagram is O.

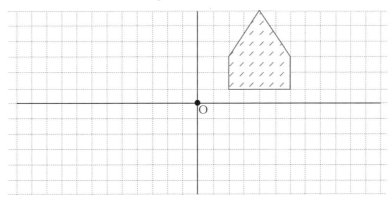

a) Rotate the shaded shape 90° clockwise. Label the new image **A**.

b) Rotate the shaded shape 180° clockwise. Label the new image **B**.

c) Rotate the shaded shape 270° clockwise. Label the new image **C**.

d) Through how many degrees clockwise would you turn image **C** to return to the position of the shaded shape?   ....

Q5   Reflect ① in the line $y = 5$, label this ②.

Reflect ② in the line $x = 9$, label this ③.

Reflect ③ in the line $y = x$, label this ④.

Reflect ④ in the line $x = 4$, label this ⑤.

Reflect ⑤ in the line $y = x$, label this ⑥.

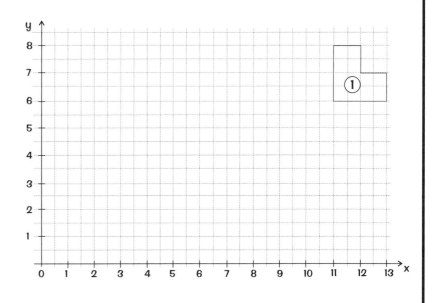

Q6   Give 6 examples of a plane of symmetry for a cube. The first one is done for you.

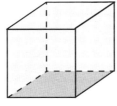
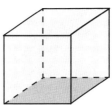

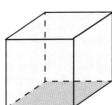
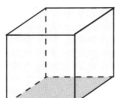
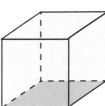

Probability and Averages

Before you start this page, work through <u>page 67</u> on probability.

Q1 When Ron and Steve play each other at snooker, the probability that Ron wins the match is 0.7. Given that a match can't end in a draw, what is the probability that Steve wins? ....

Q2 Lian's CD collection contains classical music, 90s dance, and rock ballads. She chooses a CD to listen to at random. The probability it's classical is 0.2 and the probability it's 90s dance is 0.5.

Calculate the probability that she chooses rock ballads. ....

For module 6 you need to be able to calculate averages and range, and use them to compare sets of data. See <u>page 52</u> for more questions on calculating averages, and <u>page 68</u> for more practice at using them to compare data.

Q3 Find the median, mode, mean and range of the following sets of data:

a) 20, 18, 16, 14, 12, 16, 0, 4, 6, 8

....

b) 5, 1, 2, 2, 4, 3, 3, 4, 3

....

Q4 The National Tree Service has collected data on young trees in two woods. The diameters are calculated from their circumferences to the nearest centimetre.

diameter of trees	1 - 5	6 - 10	11 - 15	16 - 20	21 - 25	26 - 30	31 - 35	Total
Acornwood	1	5	8	20	4	1	1	40
Crookthwaite	6	4	5	4	7	3	1	30

Thin tree   Fat tree

Write down the modal class for the diameters of the trees in each wood.

....

Q5 The *Doughnut Standards Agency* has been called in to inspect two doughnut stalls. They take samples of doughnuts and mark them out of 20. The marks are shown below.

Stall X	2	14	6	6	10	12	5	8	7	7
Stall Y	16	14	12	19	17	15	15	20	16	16

a) Calculate the mean and range for each of the samples.

....

b) Which doughnut stall would you recommend? Explain your answer.

....

Charts and Graphs

Q1 A baby was weighed every 5 days. The results are given below.
Draw a graph to show how the baby's weight changed.

DAY N°	0	5	10	15	20	25	30
WEIGHT KG	5.3	5.2	5.9	6.4	6.6	6.7	6.8

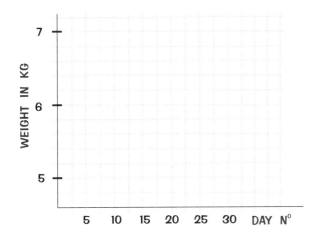

In your own words describe how
the baby's weight changed:

....

....

....

....

Q2 This stem and leaf diagram shows the exam scores of a group of Year 9 pupils.

a) How many pupils got a score between 60 and 70? ....

b) How many scored 80 or more? ....

c) What was the most common test score? ....

d) Find the median score. ....

e) Calculate the range of scores. ....

```
3 | 2 3
4 | 6 8 8
5 | 1 2 2 3 6 6 9
6 | 1 5 5 5 8
7 | 2 3 4 5 8
8 | 0 1 1 5
9 | 0 2 3
```

Key: 5 | 2 means 52

Q3 I've been measuring my friends' noses.
Here are the lengths in millimetres:

    12   18   20   11   31
    19   27   34   19   22

Complete the stem and leaf diagram on
the right to show these results.

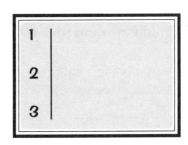

```
1 |
2 |
3 |
```

Key: 2 | 3 means 23

Frequency Tables

Q1 Last season Newcaster City played 32 matches.
The number of goals they scored in each match were recorded as shown.

2	4	3	5
1	0	3	2
4	2	1	2
0	2	3	1

1	0	0	1
1	1	1	0
1	3	2	0
1	1	0	4

Complete the tally chart and draw the frequency polygon of the goals.

GOALS	TALLY	FREQUENCY
0		
1		
2		
3		
4		
5		

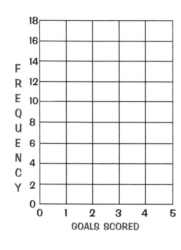

A <u>frequency polygon</u> is where you plot points for the frequencies and join them up with straight lines.

Q2 The frequency table below shows the number of hours spent Christmas shopping by 100 people surveyed in a town centre.

Number of Hours	0	1	2	3	4	5	6	7	8
Frequency	1	9	10	10	11	27	9	15	8
Hours × Frequency									

a) What is the modal number of hours spent Christmas shopping? ....

b) Fill in the third row of the table.

c) What is the total amount of time spent Christmas shopping by all the people surveyed?

....

d) What is the mean amount of time spent Christmas shopping by a person?

....

Scatter Graphs

Q1   These are the shoe sizes and heights for 12 pupils in Year 11.

Shoe size	5	6	4	6	7	7	8	3	5	9	10	10
Height (cm)	155	157	150	159	158	162	162	149	152	165	167	172

On the grid below draw a scattergraph to show this information.

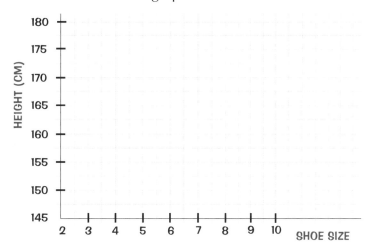

Draw a line of best fit on your scattergraph.

A line of best fit goes through the middle of the points.

What does the scattergraph tell you about the relationship between shoe size and height for these pupils?

....

Q2   This scattergraph shows how much time a group of teenagers spend on outdoor activities and playing computer games.

Which of the points A, B or C represent each of these statements?

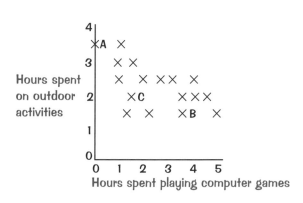

a)

Point ....

The rugby practice was a long one so I didn't have much time to play on the computer.

b)   Point ....

I don't have a computer!

c) Point ....

I went to visit a friend. We played a bit of football then spent most of the evening playing his new computer game.

MODULE 7

Powers

Random message alert... for module seven you could be asked to do <u>decimal arithmetic</u> (e.g. multiplying, dividing) without a calculator. This was covered on p72 of module 6, so have a look at that page if you think you need the practice. End of message.

Now then, **POWERS** are just a way of writing numbers in shorthand — they come in handy with big numbers. Imagine writing out 2^{138} — $2 \times 2 \times... \times 2 \times... \times 2 \times$ yawn $\times$ zzz...

Q1   Complete the following:

a) $2^4 = 2 \times 2 \times 2 \times 2 =$ ....

b) $10^3 = 10 \times 10 \times 10 =$ ....

c) $3^5 = 3\times$ .... $=$ ....

d) $4^6 = 4 \times$ .... $=$ ....

e) $1^9 = 1 \times$ .... $=$ ....

f) $5^6 = 5 \times$ .... $=$ ....

Q2   Simplify the following:

a) $2 \times 2 \times 2 \times 2 \times 2 \times 2 \times 2 \times 2 =$ ....

b) $12 \times 12 \times 12 \times 12 \times 12 =$ ....

c) $m \times m \times m =$ ....

d) $y \times y \times y \times y =$ ....

Q3   Complete the following (the first one has been done for you):

a) $10^2 \times 10^3 =$ $(10 \times 10) \times (10 \times 10 \times 10)$ $= 10^5$

b) $10^3 \times 10^4 =$ .... $=$

c) $10^4 \times 10^2 =$ .... $=$

d) What is the <u>quick method</u> for writing down the final result in **b)** and **c)**?

   ....

Q4   Complete the following (the first one has been done for you):

a) $2^4 \div 2^2 = \dfrac{(2 \times 2 \times 2 \times 2)}{(2 \times 2)} = 2^2$

c) $4^5 \div 4^3 = \dfrac{(4 \times 4 \times 4 \times 4 \times 4)}{.....................} =$ ....

b) $2^5 \div 2^2 = \dfrac{(2 \times 2 \times 2 \times 2 \times 2)}{(2 \times 2)} =$ ....

d) $8^5 \div 8^2 = \dfrac{.....................}{.....................} =$ ....

e) What is the quick method for writing down the final result in **b)**, **c)** and **d)**?

   ....

Q5   Write the following as a <u>single term</u>:

a) $10^6 \div 10^4 =$ ....

b) $(8^2 \times 8^5) \div 8^3 =$ ....

c) $6^{10} \div (6^2 \times 6^3) =$ ....

d) $x^2 \times x^3 =$ ....

e) $a^5 \times a^4 =$ ....

f) $p^4 \times p^5 \times p^6 =$ ....

Square and Cube Roots

When you have "something ^{2} = a number", you find the "something" by taking the square root of the "number". But remember, you always get a + and – answer.

E.g. $x^2 = 49$ means that $x = \pm\sqrt{49} = +7$ or -7 (because $7 \times 7 = 49$ and $-7 \times -7 = 49$).

The "$\sqrt{}$" sign means the positive square root.

Q1 Use the $\sqrt{}$ button on your calculator to find the following (positive) square roots to the nearest whole number.

a) $\sqrt{60}$ = ... e) $\sqrt{520}$ = ... i) $\sqrt{170}$ = ...

b) $\sqrt{19}$ = ... f) $\sqrt{75}$ = ... j) $\sqrt{7220}$ = ...

c) $\sqrt{34}$ = ... g) $\sqrt{750}$ = ... k) $\sqrt{1000050}$ = ...

d) $\sqrt{200}$ = ... h) $\sqrt{0.9}$ = ... l) $\sqrt{27}$ = ...

Q2 Without using a calculator, write down both answers to each of the following:

a) $x^2 = 4$ .... e) $x^2 = 25$ ....

b) $x^2 = 16$ .... f) $x^2 = 100$ ....

c) $x^2 = 9$ .... g) $x^2 = 144$ ....

d) $x^2 = 49$ .... h) $x^2 = 64$ ....

Q3 Use your calculator to find the following:

a) $\sqrt[3]{4096}$ = ... d) $\sqrt[3]{1000000}$ = ...

b) $\sqrt[3]{1728}$ = ... e) $\sqrt[3]{1}$ = ...

c) $\sqrt[3]{1331}$ = ... f) $\sqrt[3]{0.125}$ = ...

Unlike square roots, cube roots only ever have one answer.

Q4 Without using a calculator, find solve the following equations:

a) $x^3 = 64$ .... d) $x^3 = 1000$ ....

b) $x^3 = 512$ .... e) $x^3 = 216$ ....

c) $x^3 = 125$ .... f) $x^3 = 8000$ ....

Q5 A square rug has an area of 400 m². What is the length of an edge?

....

Q6 A solid cube puzzle has a volume of 343 cm³. Find the length of one of its edges.

....

Checking and Estimating

Estimating calculations is easy — just round everything off to nice, easy numbers.
Oh and <u>no calculators for this page</u> — you've got to use your own muscles...

Q1 Two of the following calculations are wrong.
By estimating the answer, decide which ones are wrong.

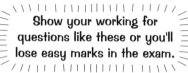

Show your working for
questions like these or you'll
lose easy marks in the exam.

a) $\dfrac{224.5 + 49.1}{53.2 - 41.2} = 228$ ....

b) $\dfrac{21 \times 11}{\sqrt{106}} = 22.4\,(3\ \text{s.f.})$ ....

c) $\dfrac{300 \times 0.8}{12 \times 2.5} = 8$ ....

d) $\dfrac{52 \times 4.8}{19^2} = 13.1\,(3\ \text{s.f.})$ ....

Q2 Estimate the values of these square roots to 1 d.p. without using a calculator:

a) 67 ....

b) 22 ....

c) 117 ....

d) 50 ....

Get off the page,
evil rocket penguin!

Q3 Explain how you can tell the calculations below are wrong without working them out.

a) $13 \times 1.3 = 11.6$ ....

b) $56 \times 236 = 780$ ....

c) $0.8 \div 1.4 = 1.2$ ....

d) $5^3 = -125$ ....

e) $25 \times -25 = 625$ ....

f) $0.8 \times 12 = 13.3$ ....

g) $\sqrt[3]{216} = 6 \text{ or } -6$ ....

Ratio and Proportion

Q1 A litre of Suzi's Strawberry Smoothy is to be divided between Dave, Dee and Daisy in the ratio 2:3:5. How many <u>millilitres</u> will each of them get?

....

Q2 Tony gives £100 to be shared by Jane, Paul and Rosemary in ratio according to their <u>age</u>. Jane is 10, Paul is 12 and Rosemary 3 years old. How much will each of them get?

....

> You can check your answer works to questions like this by adding
> up the individual amounts — they should add up to £100 here.

Q3 Now try these...

a) Adam and Mags win £24 000. They split the money in the ratio 1 : 5. How much does Adam get?

....

b) Sunil and Paul compete in a pizza eating contest. Between them they consume 28 pizzas in the ratio 3 : 4. Who wins and how many did they eat?

.... eats .... pizzas

c) The total distance covered in a triathlon (swimming, cycling and running) is 15 km. It is split in the ratio 2 : 3 : 5. How far is each section?

Swimming = ..., cycling = ..., running = ...

Q4 At Sue's Tennis Star Hair Salon, the amount that customers are charged is directly proportional to the time taken. As an example, Steffi paid £50 for a cut that took 1 hour.

a) Andre has a head polish which takes 15 minutes. How much will this cost?

....

b) Boris has a beard trim for 2.5 hours. How much will he have to pay?

....

c) Bjorn has a "short Borg and sides" which costs £65. How long did it take?

....

If this well-proportioned page of ratio delights isn't enough for you,
there's plenty more ratio practice on <u>page 71</u> of module six.

Percentages

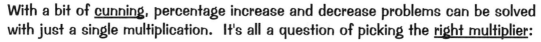

With a bit of <u>cunning</u>, percentage increase and decrease problems can be solved with just a single multiplication. It's all a question of picking the <u>right multiplier</u>:

Increase of 25%, multiplier = 1.25	Decrease of 10%, multiplier = 0.9
Increase of 5%, multiplier = 1.05	Decrease of 25%, multiplier = 0.75.

E.g. if a 10 kg cat gets 25% heavier, it will be 10 × 1.25 = 12.5 kg.
if a 10 kg cat gets 25% lighter, it will be 10 × 0.75 = 7.5 kg.

Q1 The following vegetable-inspired questions can all be solved using multipliers. For each one, write down the multiplier, then do the calculation.

a) A 5kg pumpkin increases in weight by 60% over a fortnight. Find its new weight.

Multiplier: .... Calculation: ....

b) A 15 cm tall leek increases in height by 30%. Find its new height.

Multiplier: .... Calculation: ....

c) A freshly picked radish weighs 20 g. A week later it has shrivelled up — its weight has decreased by 40%. Find its new weight.

Multiplier: .... Calculation: ....

d) Tom gets 15% lighter after eating only pumpkins, leeks and radishes for a month. If he weighed 80 kg to start with how much will he weigh now?

Multiplier: .... Calculation: ....

Q2 Charles is thinking of buying either a silly red sports car for £3000 or a sensible green people-carrier for £3700. The value of the people-carrier will depreciate by 30% each year. The sports car will hold its value better, depreciating by 20% each year.

a) How much will each car be worth in 1 year?

Silly sports car: ....

Sensible green car: ....

b) Which car will be worth more in 2 years time?

....

....

Q3 Charles buys car insurance for £600 plus a 10% fee. How much does he pay?

....

Still hungry? There are plenty more percentage questions to try on p57 (no sports cars or vegetables though). You can use the multiplier method on Q4 and Q5.

HCF, LCM and Prime Factors

The Lowest Common Multiple (LCM) is the **SMALLEST** number
that will **DIVIDE BY ALL** the numbers in question.

The Highest Common Factor (HCF) is the **BIGGEST** number
that will **DIVIDE INTO ALL** the numbers in question.

Q1 For each set of numbers find the HCF.

a) 3, 5 .... **c)** 10, 15 .... **e)** 14, 21 ....

b) 6, 8 .... **d)** 27, 48 .... **f)** 11, 33, 121 ....

Q2 For each set of numbers, find the LCM.

a) 3, 5 .... **c)** 10, 15 .... **e)** 14, 21 ....

b) 6, 8 .... **d)** 15, 18 .... **f)** 11, 33, 44 ....

Q3 Lars, Rita and Alan regularly go swimming. Lars goes every 2 days, Rita goes every 3 days and Alan goes every 5 days. They _all_ went swimming together on Friday 1st June.

a) On what _date_ will Lars and Rita next go swimming together?

....

This is a LCM question in disguise.

b) On what _date_ will Rita and Alan next go swimming together?

....

c) On what _day of the week_ will all 3 next go swimming together?

....

d) Which of the 3 (if any) will go swimming on 15th June?

....

Q4 Complete the factor trees below to express each number as a product of prime factors. The first one has been done for you.

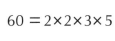
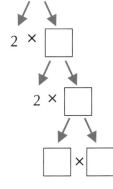
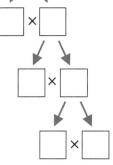

$$60 = 2 \times 2 \times 3 \times 5$$

$$88 = 2 \times 2 \times \text{........} \times \text{........}$$

$$210 = \text{........} \times \text{........} \times \text{........} \times \text{........}$$

Number Sequences

There are five special sequences: EVEN, ODD, SQUARE, CUBE and TRIANGLE NUMBERS. You really need to know them and their n^{th} terms.

Q1 Write down the next 3 terms in each of these sequences and name the type of sequence.

a) 2, 4, 6, 8, ..., ..., ...   Name of sequence: ....

b) 1, 3, 5, 7, ..., ..., ...   Name of sequence: ....

c) 1, 4, 9, 16, ..., ..., ...   Name of sequence: ....

d) 1, 8, 27, 64, ..., ..., ...   Name of sequence: ....

e) 1, 3, 6, 10, ..., ..., ...   Name of sequence: ....

They're bound to ask you to <u>find the nth term</u> in the exam, so make sure you learn the <u>formula</u>.

Q2   6   11   16   21   26 ...

a) What are the next 3 in this sequence?   ...., ..., ...

b) What is the difference between each term?   ....

c) Write down a formula for the nth term of this sequence.

....

d) Use the formula to find the 20th term of the sequence

....

Q3 Write down an expression for the nth term of the following sequences:

a) 2, 4, 6, 8, ...

....

b) 1, 3, 5, 7, ...

....

c) 5, 10, 15, 20, ...

....

OK then, I'll tell you the formula just this once: dn + (a − d) (d = difference, a = 1st term) **LEARN IT!**

d) 5, 8, 11, 14, ...

....

Equations and Formulas

Before you get going with these equations, do <u>questions 1 and 2 on page 75</u>.

Q1 Solve these equations:

a) $\frac{x}{3} + 4 = 10$

c) $4 + \frac{x}{9} = 6$

....

....

b) $\frac{x}{5} - 9 = 6$

d) $\frac{x}{17} - 11 = 31$

....

....

Q2 Solve the following:

a) $3(7 - 2x) = 2(5 - 4x)$

c) $6(x + 2) + 4(x - 3) = 50$

....

....

b) $4(3x + 2) + 3 = 3(2x - 5) + 2$

d) $10(x + 3) - 4(x - 2) = 7(x + 5)$

....

....

**You rearrange formulas in the same way as you solve equations —
keep doing the <u>opposite</u> until you get the letter you want on its own.**

Q3 Rearrange the following formulas to make the letter in brackets the new subject:

a) $y = x + 4$ (x)

d) $a = 7b + 10$ (b)

g) $y = 3x + ½$ (x)

....

....

....

b) $y = 2x + 3$ (x)

e) $w = 14 + 2z$ (z)

h) $y = 3 - x$ (x)

....

....

....

c) $y = 4x - 5$ (x)

f) $s = 4t - 3$ (t)

i) $y = 5(x + 2)$ (x)

....

....

....

Q4 Rearrange the following, to make the letter in brackets the subject of the formulas:

a) $y = \frac{x}{10}$ (x) ....

e) $f = \frac{3g}{8}$ (g) ....

b) $s = \frac{t}{14}$ (t) ....

f) $y = \frac{x}{5} + 1$ (x) ....

c) $a = \frac{2b}{3}$ (b) ....

g) $y = \frac{x}{2} - 3$ (x) ....

d) $d = \frac{3e}{4}$ (e) ....

h) $a = \frac{b}{3} - 5$ (b) ....

Equations and Formulas

Want more formula questions? You're in luck. Take a peek back at pages 43 and 75 if you want to practise some easier formula questions first.

Q5 a) To find y, multiply x by 4 and then subtract 2. Write a formula for y. ....

b) To find y, square x, add 2x and subtract 6 Write a formula for y. ....

Q6 Tickets for a football match cost £x each. Write a formula for the cost in pounds, C, of:

a) 2 tickets ....

b) n tickets ....

> CGP Wanderers Football Club
> Vs United Rovers FC
> Comfy Seat
> East stand lower bit
> Row 20
> Seat 104
> £25.00

Q7 To feed the toucans at the zoo it costs 20p, plus 50p for every bag of food you buy. Write a formula for the total cost in pence, C, of feeding the toucans with n bags of food.

....

Q8 Calculate the value of the formula $R = s^2 + 5t$ when:
a) s = 2, t = -3 ....   **b)**   s = -2, t = 3 ....

Q9 The time taken to cook a chicken is given as 20 minutes per lb plus 20 minutes extra. Find the time needed to cook a chicken weighing:

a) 4 lb   ....

b) 7.5 lb   ....

Q10 This rectangle has length l cm and width w cm. Its perimeter is p cm.

a) Write down a formula with p as the subject.   ....

b) Find the perimeter of the rectangle when l = 12 and w = 5.

....

c) Rearrange your formula from part **a)** to make l the subject. ....

Q11 A car sales person is paid £w for working m months and selling c cars, where w = 500m + 50c.

a) Rearrange the formula to make c the subject. ....

b) Find the number of cars the sales person sells in 11 months if he earns £12,100 during that time. ....

Algebra

The best way to multiply two brackets together is to use the <u>FOIL</u> method — <u>F</u>irsts, <u>O</u>utsides, <u>I</u>nsides, <u>L</u>asts.

Q1 For each of the large rectangles below, write down the area of the four smaller rectangles.

a)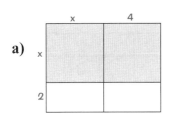

.... ' ....

.... ' ....

b)

.... ' ....

.... ' ....

c)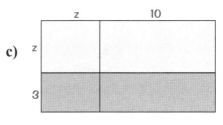

.... ' ....

.... ' ....

Q2 Multiply out the brackets and simplify your answers where possible:

a) $(x + 4)(x + 2)$

....

b) $(y + 8)(y + 5)$

....

c) $(z + 10)(z + 3)$

....

(Use your answers to **Q1** to help you check you've multiplied out the brackets correctly.)

Q3 Expand these brackets and simplify:

a) $(x + 1)(x + 2) =$

....

b) $(x + 3)(x + 2) =$

....

c) $(x + 4)(x + 5) =$

....

d) $(x + 5)(x - 1) =$

....

e) $(2x + 2)(x - 3) =$

....

f) $(x - 3)(3x + 1) =$

....

Quadratic Graphs

If an expression has an x^2 term as the highest power, it's quadratic. The graphs you get from quadratic expressions are always curves with a certain shape.

Q1 Complete this table of values for the quadratic graph $y = 2x^2$.

a) On the graph paper below, draw axes with x from -4 to 4 and y from 0 to 32.

x	-4	-3	-2	-1	0	1	2	3	4
$y=2x^2$	32	18					8		

Remember to square first then x 2

b) Plot the 9 points and join them with a smooth curve.

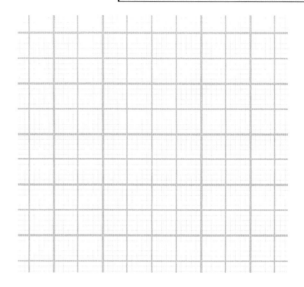

Q2 Complete this table of values for the graph $y = x^2 + x$.

x	-4	-3	-2	-1	0	1	2	3	4
x^2	16	9					4		
$y=x^2+x$	12					2			

By putting more steps in your table of values, the arithmetic is easier

a) On the graph paper, draw axes with x from -4 to 4 and y from 0 to 20.

b) Plot the points and join them with a smooth curve.

c) Use your graph to find the two solutions of the equation $x^2 + x = 0$.

x = ... or ....

Just find the x-values where the graph crosses the x-axis (i.e. where y = 0).

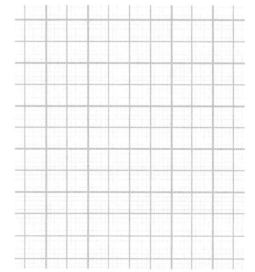

Quadratic Graphs

 You'll need some graph paper for the next three questions.

Q3 a) Complete this table of values for the graph $y = x^2 - 4x + 1$.

x	-2	-1	0	1	2	3	4
x^2	4	1				9	
-4x	8					-12	
1	1	1				1	
$y=x^2-4x+1$	13	6				-2	

b) Plot the graph $y = x^2 - 4x + 1$, using axes with x from -2 to 5 and y from -3 to 13.

c) Use your graph to find approximate solutions of the equation $x^2 - 4x + 1 = 0$.

x = ... or ....

If the x^2 term has a <u>minus</u> sign in front of it, the bucket will be turned <u>upside down</u>.

Q4 a) Complete this table of values for the graph $y = 3 - x^2$.

x	-4	-3	-2	-1	0	1	2	3	4
3	3	3	3	3	3	3	3	3	3
$-x^2$	-16						-4		
$y=3-x^2$	-13						-1		

b) Draw the graph $y = 3 - x^2$ for x from -4 to 4.

c) Use your graph to find approximate solutions of the equation $3 - x^2 = 0$.

x = ... or ....

Q5 a) Draw the graph $y = -x^2 + x + 4$ for values of x from -3 to 4.

b) Use your graph to find approximate solutions to the equation $-x^2 + x + 4 = 0$

x = ... or ....

If any points look a bit strange, check you've got them right in the <u>table of values</u>. I know it's boring doing it all again, but it shouldn't be too hard if you've put all the steps in. And it'll mean you <u>don't get it wrong</u>. Which is always nice.

Inequalities

Yet another one of those bits of Maths that looks worse than it is — these are just like equations, really, except for the symbols.

Q1   Write down an inequality for each of the diagrams below.

a)  ....

b) ....

c) ....

d) 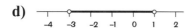 ....

e) 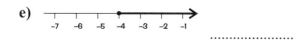 ....

f) ....

g) 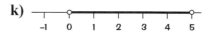 ....

h) ....

i)  ....

j) ....

k) ....

l) ....

Q2   Solve the following inequalities:

a) $2x \geqslant 16$ ....

b) $4x > -20$ ....

c) $x + 2 > 5$ ....

d) $x - 3 \leqslant 10$ ....

e) $x + 4 \geqslant 14$ ....

f) $10x > -2$ ....

g) $5 + x \geqslant 12$ ....

h) $x/4 > 10$ ....

i) $x/3 \leqslant 1$ ....

j) $x/2 \leqslant 4$ ....

Q3   There are 1,130 pupils in a school and no classes have more than 32 pupils. What is the least number of classrooms that could be used? Show this information as an inequality.

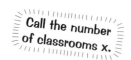

Call the number of classrooms x.

....

Trial and Improvement

Q1 Use the trial and improvement method to solve the equation $x^3 = 50$.
Give your answer to one decimal place. Two trials have been done for you.

Try $x = 3$, $x^3 = 27$ (too small)
Try $x = 4$, $x^3 = 64$ (too big)

Oh, sorry. I was looking for page 110.

....

Q2 Use the trial and improvement method to solve these equations.
Give your answers to one decimal place.

a) $x^2 + x = 80$

....

b) $x^3 - x = 100$

....

Show all the numbers you've tried, not just your final answer...
or you'll be chucking away easy marks.

Circles — Area and Circumference

Remember — π just stands for the number **3.14159...** Use the π button on your calculator unless the question tells you to leave your answer "in terms of π".

Q1 A plant is in a pot. The radius of the top of the pot is 4.5 cm.
Calculate the circumference of the top of the pot.

....

Q2 The circumference of a circle is 195 cm.
Calculate its diameter correct to 3 s.f.

Diameter = ...

Q3 Calculate the area of each circle.
Write your answers to **a)** and **b)** as multiples of π.

a)

Area = π × radius² = ...

b) A circle of radius 9 cm. Area = π × radius² = ...

Q4 Find the area of one face of a 10p coin, radius 1.2 cm.
Give your answer correct to 3 s.f.

Area = ...

Q5 A circular table has a diameter of 50 cm.
Find the area of the table to 3 s.f.

Area = ...

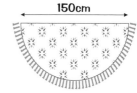

150cm

Q6 What is the area of this semicircular rug?
Give your answer to the nearest whole number.

Area = ...

Q7 This circular pond has a circular path around it. The radius of the pond is 72 m and the
path is 2 m wide. Calculate to the nearest whole number:

the area of the pond ....

the area of the path ....

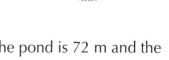

path

pond

Q8 In Q7, the radius is given as 72 m, rounded off to the nearest whole metre.
What are the least and greatest distances it could have been?

Least: .... Greatest: ....

Circles — Geometry Problems

 Remember these 2 rules for circle geometry problems:

1) ANGLE FORMED IN A SEMI-CIRCLE = 90°

2) ANGLE BETWEEN TANGENT AND RADIUS = 90°

Q1 In the diagram to the right, O is the centre of the circle and AB is a tangent to the circle.

a) State the size of angle w and give a reason for your answer.

....

b) Work out angle x:

....

c) Work out angle y:

....

Q2 In the diagram, O is the centre of the circle and P is the point where the tangent shown meets the circle. Find angle z:

....

....

Before you try the last question, make sure you can do the parallel lines questions on page 78 of module six.

Q3 In the diagram shown, O is the centre of the circle and DF is a tangent to the circle.

a) State the size of angle w. Explain your answer.

....

....

b) Work out angle x. Show your working.

....

c) State the size of angle y. Explain your answer.

....

d) Work out angle z. Show your working.

....

Pythagoras' Theorem

If you're as big a fan of Pythagoras as me, you'll ignore him and use this method instead:

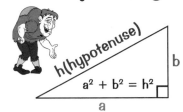

1) **SQUARE** the two numbers that you are given.
2) To find the <u>longest side, **ADD**</u> the two squared numbers.
   To find a <u>shorter side, **SUBTRACT**</u> the smaller one from the larger.
3) Take the **SQUARE ROOT**. Then check that your answer is sensible.

Q1 Using Pythagoras' theorem, calculate the length of the third side
in these triangles, giving your answers to <u>3 significant figures</u>.

$c^2 =$ .... + ... = ..., $c =$ ....

$d^2 =$ .... + ... = ..., $d =$ ....

$e^2 =$ .... − .... = ..., $e =$ ....

$f^2 =$ .... − .... = ..., $f =$ ....

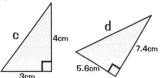

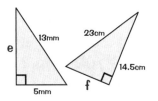

Q2 Using Pythagoras' theorem, work out which of these triangles have right-angles.

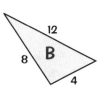

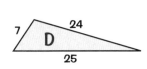

If they don't have right-angles, the numbers won't fit the formula.

....

....

Q3 Calculate the missing lengths in these quadrilaterals. Give your answers to 3 sig. figs.

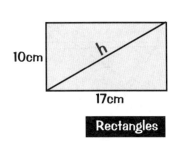
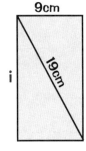
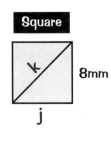
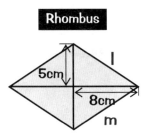

$h =$ ...., $i =$ ....,

$j =$ ...., $k =$ ....,

$l =$ ...., $m =$ ....

Volume and Surface Area

Contrary to popular belief, there isn't anything that complicated about prisms — they're only solids with the same shape all the way through. To find the volume, just <u>multiply the cross-sectional area by the length</u>. The only bit that sometimes takes a bit longer is finding the cross-sectional area.

Q1 Rubber chocks are put under the wheels of aeroplanes to stop them moving when on the ground. A typical chock is shown.

a) Calculate the volume of the chock.

....

....

b) Calculate its surface area.

....

....

....

> The surface area is made up of 2 identical trapeziums + 4 different rectangles.

> You'll need to use Pythagoras to find the sloping length.

20cm
35cm
50cm
40cm

Q2 Bill bought a new garden shed with dimensions as shown.

Find:

a) the area of the cross-section

....

....

b) the volume of the shed

....

c) the length AB

....

....

> You'll need Pythagoras again here to find the length AB.

d) the total area of the roof.

....

4 m
5 m
2.5 m
E
A
B
D
4 m
C

Volume and Surface Area

Q3   Joe buys a garden cloche to protect his plants from frost.
It has a semicircular diameter of 70 cm and a length of 3 m.

3 m

70 cm

a) Find the cross-sectional area.

....

b) Hence find the volume of the cloche.

....

c) Find the surface area of the cloche (not including the base).

....

....

Q4   A cylindrical copper pipe has insulation in the form
of a foam tube placed around the outside of it. The
pipe has external dimensions of 10 cm diameter and
10 m length. The foam tubing is 1 cm thick

10 m

1 cm

10 cm

Insulation
Copper

a) Find the <u>cross-sectional area</u> of insulation.

....

....

....

*Work out the area of the
inner pipe and the area of
the pipe with insulation,
then just subtract them.*

b) Find the <u>volume</u> of the insulation over the 10 m length.
Give your answer in m^3.

....

Q5   A really really big coffee mug is a cylinder closed at one end.
The internal radius is 7 cm and the internal height is 9 cm.

a) Taking π to be 3.14, find the volume of liquid the mug can hold.

....

b) If 1200 cm^3 of liquid is poured into the mug, find the depth to the nearest whole cm.

....

....

*To find the depth, d, of the
liquid you need to rearrange
the volume formula ($V = \pi r^2 d$)
to get d on its own.*

Coordinates

Q1 Find the midpoint of the line segments AB, where A and B have coordinates:

a) A(2,3)   B(4,5)   ....

d) A(3,15)   B(13,3)   ....

b) A(1,8)   B(9,2)   ....

e) A(6,6)   B(0,0)   ....

c) A(0,11)   B(12,11)   ....

f) A(15,9)   B(3,3)   ....

Your answers should be coordinates too.

ahh... nice'n'easy...

Q2 Find the midpoint of each of the line segments on this graph.

AB: ....

CD: ....

EF: ....

GH: ....

JK: ....

LM: ....

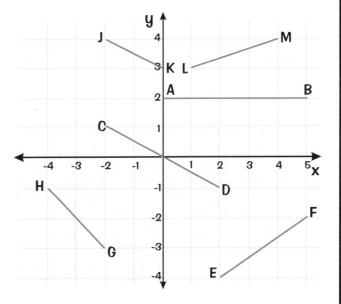

Q3 The diagram shows a cuboid. Vertices A and H have coordinates (1, 2, 8) and (4, 5, 3) respectively. Write down the coordinates of all the other vertices.

B (.... , ... , ...)

C (.... , ... , ...)

D (.... , ... , ...)

E (.... , ... , ...)

F (.... , ... , ...)

G (.... , ... , ...)

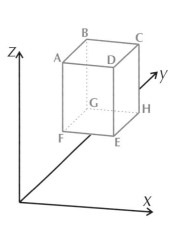

Loci and Constructions

Work through these questions bit by bit, and remember the following...

> **LOCUS** — a line showing all points obeying the given rule.
> **BISECTOR** — a line splitting an angle or line exactly in two.

Q1 **a)** In the space to the left, construct a triangle ABC with AB = 4 cm, BC = 5 cm, AC = 3 cm.

b) Construct the perpendicular bisector of AB and where this line meets BC, label the new point D.

c) Measure the length BD.

Q2 In the middle of the space below, mark two points A and B which are 6 cm apart.

a) Draw the locus of points which are 4 cm from A.

b) Draw the locus of points which are 3 cm from B.

c) There are 2 points which are both 4 cm from A and 3 cm from B. Label them X and Y.

Loci and Constructions

Q3 Two churches with bell towers are 2 km apart. On a still day, the sound of the bells can be heard 1.5 km away. To the right, draw an accurate diagram to show the two churches, and for each one, draw the locus of points where its bell can be heard. Shade the area where <u>both</u> bells can be heard.

Suggested scale: 1 cm = 1 km

Q4 Tony likes to look at the tree in his garden. The diagram to the right shows the position of the tree relative to his bedroom window. Tony wants to position his bed in such a way that he can see the tree in the morning as he awakes.

Carefully <u>shade</u> on the diagram the area in which Tony could position his bed.

He doesn't need to be able to see the whole tree.

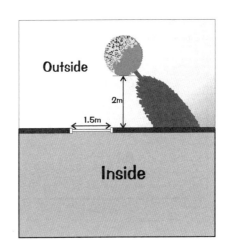

Outside

2m

1.5m

Inside

Q5

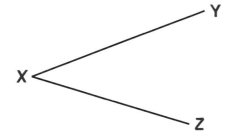

Y

X

Z

The diagram on the left shows two lines XY and XZ which meet at the point X. Construct the angle bisector of YXZ.

Speed

This is an easy enough formula — and of course you can put it in that good old formula triangle as well.

Average speed = $\dfrac{\text{Total distance}}{\text{Total time}}$

Q1   A train travels 240 km in 4 hours. What is its <u>average speed</u>?

....

Q2   A car travels for 3 hours at an average speed of 55 mph. How far has it travelled?

....

Q3   <u>Complete</u> this table.

Distance Travelled	Time taken	Average Speed
210 km	3 hrs	
135 miles		30 mph
	2 hrs 30 mins	42 km/h
9 miles	45 mins	
640 km		800 km/h
	1 hr 10 mins	60 mph

Q4   An athlete can run 100 m in 11 seconds.
Calculate the athlete's speed in:

a) m/s

....

b) km/h

....

Q5   A plane flies over city A at 09.55 and over city B at 10.02.
What is its <u>average</u> speed if these cities are 63 miles apart?

....

Q6   The distance from Kendal (Oxenholme) to London (Euston) is 280 miles. The train travels at an average speed of 63 mph. If I catch the 07.05 from Kendal, can I be at a meeting in London by 10.30? <u>Show all your working</u>.

....

Density

Here we go again — the multi-purpose formula triangle. Learn the positions of M, D and V, plug in the numbers and pull out the answer... magic.

$$\text{DENSITY} = \frac{\text{mass}}{\text{volume}}$$

M / D × V

Q1   Find the <u>density</u> of each of these pieces of wood, giving your answer in g/cm³:

a) Mass 3 g, volume 4 cm³

....

b) Mass 20 g, volume 25 cm³

....

c) Mass 12 kg, volume 20,000 cm³

....

d) Mass 14 kg, volume 0.02 m³.

....

Q2   Calculate the <u>mass</u> of each of these objects:

a) a small marble statue of density
2.6 g/cm³ and volume 24 cm³   ....

b) a plastic cube of volume 64 cm³
and density 1.5 g/cm³   ....

c) a gold ingot with density 19.5 g/cm³
measuring 12 cm by 4 cm by 4 cm   ....

d) a pebble with volume 30 cm³
and density 2.5 g/cm³.   ....

Q3   Work out the <u>volume</u> of each of these items:

a) a bag of sugar of mass 1 kg and density 1.6 g/cm³

....

b) a packet of margarine with density 2.8 g/cm³ and mass 250 g

....

c) a 50 kg sack of coal with density 1.8 g/cm³

....

d) a box of cereal with density 0.2 g/cm³ and mass 500 g.

....

Q4   Ice has a density of 0.93 g/cm³.
If the mass of a block of ice is 19.5 kg, what is its <u>volume</u>?

....

Probability — Relative Frequency

You need to be able to <u>calculate</u> *and* <u>estimate</u> probabilities for module 7. So have a go at <u>page 67</u> on calculating probabilities before you start on relative frequency.

Q1 **a)** A biased dice is rolled 40 times. A six came up 14 times.
Calculate the relative frequency that a six was rolled.

....

b) The same dice is rolled another 60 times. From this, a six came up 24 times.
Calculate the relative frequency that a six was rolled.

....

c) Use the data from **a)** and **b)** to make the best estimate you
can of the probability of rolling a six with the dice.

....

*Remember — the more
times you do an experiment,
the more accurate it will be.*

Q2 The notepad below shows orders for 4 different sorts of rice at a certain Indian
restaurant. Based on this data, estimate the probability that the next order of rice is:

a) for pilau rice? ....

b) for spicy mushroom or special fried rice? ....

c) not for boiled rice? ....

boiled	20
pilau	24
spicy mushroom	10
special fried	6

*If you're asked to work out probabilities based on
some data, it's a <u>relative frequency</u> question.*

Q3 Imagine you have just made a 6-sided spinner in Design and Technology.
How could you test whether or not it's a fair spinner?

*Remember — if the spinner's
fair, the probability of landing
on each side is the same.*

....

....

....

....

Grouped Frequency Tables

First things first, do __page 88__ on standard frequency tables.
Done that? Good. Now here are some trickier questions,
where you have to __estimate__ the mean using mid-interval values.

Q1 In a survey of test results in a French class at Blugdon High,
these grades were achieved by the 23 pupils:

(grade) score	(E) 31-40	(D) 41-50	(C) 51-60	(B) 61-70
frequency	4	7	8	4

a) Write down the mid-interval values
for each of the groups.

....

b) Calculate an estimate for the mean value.

....

....

Q2 This table shows times for each team of swimmers, the Dolphins and the Sharks.

Dolphins			Sharks		
Time interval (seconds)	Frequency	Mid-interval value	Time interval (seconds)	Frequency	Mid-interval value
$14 \leq t < 20$	3	17	$14 \leq t < 20$	6	17
$20 \leq t < 26$	7	23	$20 \leq t < 26$	15	23
$26 \leq t < 32$	15		$26 \leq t < 32$	33	
$32 \leq t < 38$	32		$32 \leq t < 38$	59	
$38 \leq t < 44$	45		$38 \leq t < 44$	20	
$44 \leq t < 50$	30		$44 \leq t < 50$	8	
$50 \leq t < 56$	5		$50 \leq t < 56$	2	

a) Complete the table, writing in all mid-interval values.

b) Use the mid-interval technique to estimate the mean time for each team.

....

....

....

Scatter Graphs

Q1 The scattergraphs below show the relationship between:

a) The temperature of the day and the amount of ice cream sold.

b) The price of ice cream and the amount sold.

c) The age of customers and the amount of ice cream sold.

a) 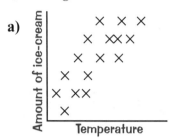 b)  c)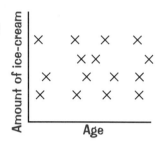

Describe the correlation of each graph and say what each graph tells you.

a)

....

b)

....

c)

....

Q2 **a)** Alice wants to buy a second hand car. She looks in the local paper and writes down the ages and prices of 15 cars. On the grid below draw a scattergraph for Alice's information.

Age of car (years)	Price (£)
4	4995
2	7995
3	6595
1	7995
5	3495
8	4595
9	1995
1	7695
2	7795
6	3995
5	3995
1	9195
3	5995
4	4195
9	2195

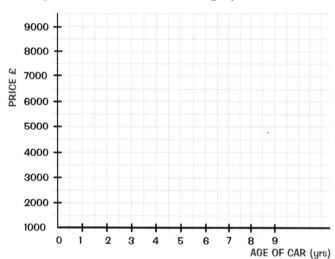

b) What does the scattergraph tell you about the relationship between the age of a car and its price?

....

c) Draw a line of best fit on the scatter graph and use it to estimate the price of a second hand car which is 7 years old.

....

Congratulations, you've reached the end of the book! Before you go, here is one final piece of wisdom to take with you... Beware of penguins — they pretend to be friends, then eat you.